Adapted an[d]
IAN DAVI[DSON]

MARVIN

Based on "The Way I Was"
by MARVIN HAMLISCH
with Gerald Gardner

Schiffer **Kids**

4880 Lower Valley Road, Atglen, PA 19310

Type set in Anime Ace 2

ISBN: 978-0-7643-5904-0
Printed in China

Published by Schiffer Kids
An imprint of Schiffer Publishing, Ltd.
4880 Lower Valley Road
Atglen, PA 19310
Phone: (610) 593-1777; Fax: (610) 593-2002
E-mail: Info@schifferbooks.com
Web: www.schifferbooks.com

For our complete selection of fine books on this and related subjects, please visit our website at www.schifferbooks.com. You may also write for a free catalog.

Schiffer Publishing's titles are available at special discounts for bulk purchases for sales promotions or premiums. Special editions, including personalized covers, corporate imprints, and excerpts, can be created in large quantities for special needs. For more information, contact the publisher.

I WAS SIX YEARS OLD WHEN I WAS USHERED INTO THE ADMISSIONS TEST FOR THE JUILLIARD SCHOOL OF MUSIC.

THERE I AM, IN MY SAILOR SUIT, FACING THREE TALL MEN.

(EVERYBODY LOOKS TALL WHEN YOU'RE SIX)

MARVIN, WILL YOU BE PLAYING ANY MOZART FOR US? OR POSSIBLY CLEMENTI?

NO! I DON'T KNOW WHO CLEMENTI IS, AND I NEVER STUDIED MOZART.

THEN WHAT *WILL* YOU BE PLAYING FOR US?

WELL, I LISTEN TO THE RADIO A LOT. I CAN PLAY "GOODNIGHT IRENE."

HMM!

WELL I DON'T KNOW "GOODNIGHT IRENE."

THAT'S ALL RIGHT. I CAN PLAY IT IN ANY KEY YOU WANT!

AND THOSE WERE THE KEYS THAT OPENED THE LOCK OF THE JUILLIARD SCHOOL OF MUSIC.

YOU HAVE TO UNDERSTAND MORE ABOUT MY PARENTS TO KNOW WHY THEY ENROLLED ME IN THE PREPARATORY DIVISION AT AGE SIX, THE YOUNGEST STUDENT EVER TO WALK THOSE HALLOWED HALLS.

THEY WERE FROM VIENNA, AND MY FATHER, MAX, *LOVED* VIENNA.

MAX WAS A TRUE VIENNESE *GENTLEMAN*-- THE SORT WHO KISSED LADIES' HANDS.

GNÄDIGE FRAU!

HE LOVED OLD WORLD CULTURE; THE MUSIC OF SCHUBERT, SCHUMANN, AND STRAUSS; THE CAFES; THE INCREDIBLE DESSERTS...

Juden Zutritt verboten!

MAX WOULD CERTAINLY HAVE STAYED THERE IF HITLER HADN'T HAD *OTHER IDEAS.*

ARRIVING IN AMERICA AND NOT BEING FLUENT IN ENGLISH, HE FOUND IT HARD TO COPE WITH THIS FRANTIC NEW LAND.

LIKE MOST VIENNESE, INSTEAD OF TRYING TO ADAPT TO NEW YORK, HE DECIDED TO REPLICATE VIENNA HERE.

MY FATHER HAD BEEN ON HIS WAY TO A SUCCESSFUL CAREER AS A MUSICIAN IN VIENNA.

IN HIS EYES, JUILLIARD WAS WHERE GOD LEARNED TO PLAY THE SCALES.

IF JUILLIARD WAS GOOD ENOUGH FOR GOD, IT JUST MIGHT BE GOOD ENOUGH FOR MARVIN FREDERICK HAMLISCH, BORN JUNE 2, 1944.

SO WHEN THE LETTER ARRIVED TO SAY THAT MAX'S LITTLE BOY HAD BEEN ACCEPTED TO JUILLIARD, YOU WOULD HAVE THOUGHT WE HAD WON FIRST PRIZE IN THE PUBLISHERS CLEARING HOUSE GIVEAWAY.

MY FATHER WAS INSTANTLY TRANSFORMED FROM A POOR AUSTRIAN IMMIGRANT INTO THE IMPOSSIBLY PROUD FATHER OF A JUILLIARD STUDENT.

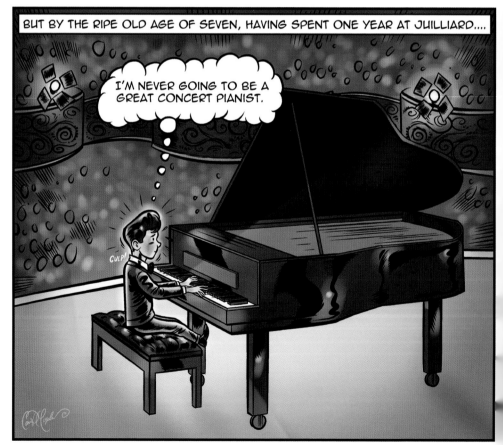

BUT BY THE RIPE OLD AGE OF SEVEN, HAVING SPENT ONE YEAR AT JUILLIARD....

I'M NEVER GOING TO BE A GREAT CONCERT PIANIST.

GULP!

JUILLIARD'S PRIMARY INTENTION WAS TO MAKE THEIR STUDENTS GREAT INSTRUMENTALISTS –

ANYTHING ELSE, LIKE COMPOSING FOR THE THEATER, WAS NOT FOR THEM.

JUILLIARD WAS GOING TO MAKE ME THE NEXT HOROWITZ WHETHER I LIKED IT OR NOT. BUT I DID NOT WANT TO PRACTICE THAT MUCH.

I DIDN'T HAVE THE TECHNICAL ABILITY OR CONFIDENCE. I WAS MUCH TOO *NERVOUS* FOR IT.

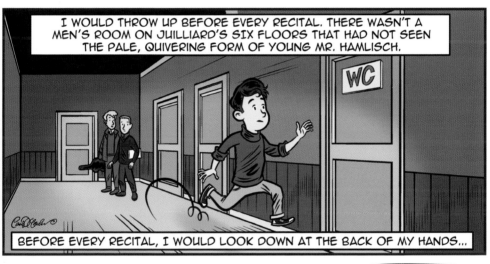

I WOULD THROW UP BEFORE EVERY RECITAL. THERE WASN'T A MEN'S ROOM ON JUILLIARD'S SIX FLOORS THAT HAD NOT SEEN THE PALE, QUIVERING FORM OF YOUNG MR. HAMLISCH.

BEFORE EVERY RECITAL, I WOULD LOOK DOWN AT THE BACK OF MY HANDS...

...AND SEE THE VIVID BLUE OF MY BULGING VEINS LIKE A...

...ROAD MAP TO TERROR!

THE JITTERY NERVES AND ACID STOMACH HAVE DOGGED ME EVER SINCE I BEGAN AT THAT SCHOOL!

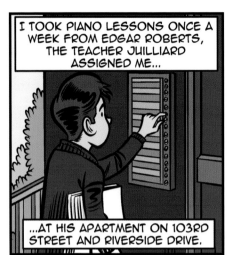

I TOOK PIANO LESSONS ONCE A WEEK FROM EDGAR ROBERTS, THE TEACHER JUILLIARD ASSIGNED ME...

...AT HIS APARTMENT ON 103RD STREET AND RIVERSIDE DRIVE.

I ALSO ATTENDED P.S. 9 FROM NINE TO THREE EACH DAY, AND THEN ON SATURDAY, WHILE MY FRIENDS WERE PLAYING STICKBALL, I'D REPORT TO JUILLIARD, WHERE I ATTENDED CLASSES IN THEORY, SIGHT READING, AND HARMONY.

MIND YOU, I AM NOT PLEADING CHILD ABUSE. I DID SEE *HOPALONG CASSIDY* ON TV...

HOPALONG CASSIDY

...AND PLAYED MY SHARE OF STICKBALL.

WHACK!

I ADAPTED AND DEVELOPED A NEW PHILOSOPHY. I WAS ONLY GOING TO DREAD *ONE DAY AT A TIME.*

I HAD TO INVENT AN ASSORTMENT OF EXCUSES TO GET UP FROM "FÜR ELISE."

MAAAX! I THINK MARVIN HAS A *BLADDER INFECTION!!*

STILL, HOW MANY TIMES CAN YOU GO TO THE BATHROOM?

BY NOW, MY FATHER COULD TELL SOMETHING WAS LACKING IN MY DEDICATION...

MAAAAAAX! I THINK MARVIN HAS A BLADDER INFECTION *AGAIN!!*

SO HE CONCOCTED A SCHEME TO TURN LEMONS INTO LEMONADE.

HE DESIGNED A HOMEMADE DECK OF CARDS. HE TOOK OUT A PROTRACTOR AND MEASURED THE CARDS...

Practice the Chopin for 10 Minutes! again

Do a G-Flat Major Scale

...SO THEY'D BE THE SAME SIZE AS OFFICIAL PLAYING CARDS. AND ON THE BACK OF EACH ONE IT WOULD SAY *MARVIN.*

I WOULD PICK A CARD AND HAVE TO FOLLOW THE DIRECTIONS ON IT. THE TRICK WAS, ONE CARD READ...

Ten Minute Break!

OF COURSE, UNKNOWN TO MY FATHER, I HAD MARKED THE CARDS. I KNEW WHERE THAT BREAK CARD WAS ALL THE TIME...

Marvin

...EVENTUALLY, I WAS FOUND OUT, BUT FOR A BRIEF, SHINING MOMENT, I HAD COMMITTED THE *PERFECT CRIME.*

SOMETIMES I HAD HOURS TO KILL BETWEEN THE SCHEDULED SATURDAY MUSIC CLASSES. RATHER THAN TRAVEL FROM 122ND STREET AND BROADWAY (WHERE JUILLIARD WAS LOCATED IN THOSE DAYS) TO OUR APARTMENT AND BACK, I WOULD HUNT FOR ONE OF THE PRACTICE ROOMS AT SCHOOL.

A LOT OF OTHER STUDENTS ALSO SOUGHT OUT THESE ROOMS TO GET IN SOME EXTRA STUDY TIME. PIANISTS, CELLISTS, AND VIOLISTS ROAMED THE HALLS IN WOLF PACKS. THESE ROOMS HAD DOUBLE DOORS. THE IDEA WAS THAT IF YOU WERE PLAYING THE PIANO LOUDLY, THE FLUTIST NEXT DOOR WOULDN'T BE DISTURBED.

ON THOSE DAYS WHEN I WAS LUCKY ENOUGH TO FIND A PRACTICE ROOM, I KNEW THAT THE ROOM TO MY RIGHT WAS PROBABLY BEING USED BY A BRILLIANT PROTÉGÉ WORKING FEVERISHLY ON A DIFFICULT BEETHOVEN SONATA.

THE ROOM TO MY LEFT, NO DOUBT, HAD SOME EIGHT-YEAR-OLD JAPANESE VIOLINIST PERFECTING SOME ULTRACOMPLICATED CADENZA.

BOTH OF THEM OBLIVIOUS TO THE FACT THAT I WAS PLAYING...

TEARS ON MY PILLOW!

...A FIFTIES ROCK-AND-ROLL SONG!

THERE I'D BE, PLAYING JUST BECAUSE I LOVED TO PLAY...

NOTHING!

AND THANKS TO THOSE MIRACULOUS DOUBLE DOORS...

WANTED DEAD OR ALIVE FUGITIVE MUSICIAN PLAYER AND COMPOSER OF POP TUNES

...MY GUILTY SECRET REMAINED MINE ALONE. MARVIN, THE FUGITIVE MUSICIAN, PLAYER AND COMPOSER OF POP TUNES.

BY NOW, I HAD HIDDEN AWAY A STACK FULL OF MY OWN SONGS.

MIND YOU, I AM NOT SUGGESTING THAT YOU ADOPT A LIFE OF DECEPTION, CONCEALMENT, AND MISREPRESENTATION. BUT IT'S ALWAYS WORKED FOR ME.

ONCE A YEAR EVERY JUILLIARD STUDENT TOOK A PROFICIENCY EXAMINATION. THE TEST WOULD DETERMINE WHETHER WE KEPT OUR SCHOLARSHIP FOR THE FOLLOWING YEAR.

IN MY CASE, IT WAS AN ABSOLUTE MUST, SINCE MY PARENTS COULDN'T AFFORD THE TUITION. THE EXAM TOOK PLACE IN FRONT OF THE PEOPLE THEY CALLED THE JURY. (HAS A NICE RING TO IT: LIKE "CONVICTED ON ALL COUNTS.")

THE ANNUAL RECITAL EXAM ALWAYS CAME SHORTLY AFTER MY BIRTHDAY AND TOTALLY SPOILED THE EVENT.

IT WOULD MAKE MY BIRTHDAY A DISASTER. HOW COULD I ENJOY CAKE, COOKIES, AND PRESENTS WHEN TWO DAYS LATER I WOULD HAVE TO FACE THE *FIRING SQUAD*?

FOR THE EXAMINATION, WE HAD TO PRESENT A TYPE-WRITTEN LIST OF THE PIECES WE WERE PREPARED TO PLAY, ENTER A WINDOWLESS ROOM THAT HAD NOTHING IN IT BUT A PIANO AND THREE JUDGES, HAND THEM THE LIST, AND STAND THERE IN AGONY, WAITING TILL THEY DECIDED WHAT THEY WANTED TO HEAR. THEY USUALLY CHOSE THE MOST DIFFICULT PART OF EACH PIECE. NATURALLY.

FOR ME THERE WAS AN EVEN BIGGER PROBLEM. PRESENTING THEM WITH THE TYPEWRITTEN LIST PROVED FORMIDABLE IN ITSELF. *WE DIDN'T OWN A TYPEWRITER!*

CLACK! CLACK! CLACK!

I'D USUALLY START THE DAY BY THROWING UP. AND THAT WAS THE HIGH POINT OF THE DAY.

W.C.

(IT NEVER GOT ANY BETTER IN THE FOURTEEN YEARS I ATTENDED JUILLIARD.)

MY MOTHER WOULD GIVE ME NOTHING BUT WEAK CHAMOMILE TEA...

...OR I WOULD SIP SHOT GLASSES OF MAALOX.

I WOULD THINK ABOUT THE HOURS AFTER THE EXAM WHEN I'D BE ABLE TO JOIN MY FRIENDS AND PLAY BASEBALL.

THERE WOULD BE NO FURTHER NEED TO PROTECT MY HANDS.

THE SUMMER WOULD COME, AND I'D BE FREE TILL SEPTEMBER.

BUT FREEDOM PASSED QUICKLY, AND BEFORE I KNEW IT, IT WAS TIME TO SURVIVE ANOTHER EXAMINATION AND THEN BE ALLOWED TO RETURN TO THE HALLOWED HALLS.

GULP!

THE WORST EXAM RECITAL I CAN REMEMBER WAS AT AGE TEN. MY MOTHER BOUGHT ME MY FIRST GRAY WOOL SUIT FOR THE OCCASION FROM RAPPOPORT'S AT EIGHTY-THIRD AND BROADWAY.

THE DAY OF MY EXAM WAS THE FIRST TIME I WORE THE SUIT. THE PANTS ITCHED TOO MUCH. THE WOOL WAS DRIVING ME NUTS.

SCRATCH! SCRATCH!

AS USUAL, MY MOTHER HAD A SOLUTION. THERE WAS NO TIME TO GET ANOTHER SUIT AND NO TIME TO STITCH A LINING IN THIS ONE.

MARVIN, PUT ON YOUR PAJAMA BOTTOMS UNDERNEATH!

THE ONES WITH THE LITTLE BEARS AND INDIANS...

ALL DAY, ALONG WITH MY USUAL DREAD OF FLUNKING THE EXAM AND LOSING MY SCHOLARSHIP (AND MY BREAKFAST), I CARRIED THE SECRET FEAR THAT MY HUMILIATING *PAJAMA-PANTS SECRET* WOULD SOMEHOW BE DISCOVERED.

BUT THAT DAY HAD GREATER TERRORS IN STORE. MY FATHER, ALWAYS A CAUTIOUS MAN, INSISTED WE LEAVE THE HOUSE WITH AMPLE TIME TO SPARE. SO WE ARRIVED AT SCHOOL WITH A FULL HOUR TO KILL. THE WAITING WAS HELL. TO HELP ME THROUGH THE INTERMINABLE SIXTY MINUTES, MY FATHER DECIDED WE WOULD EXPLORE THE JUILLIARD BUILDING. THAT WAS A LITTLE LIKE TAKING ANNE BOLEYN ON A TOUR OF THE TOWER TO KEEP HER MIND OFF WHAT LAY AHEAD. FIRST WE PACED THE HALLWAYS OF ALL SIX FLOORS. THEN WE EXPLORED A FEW EMPTY CLASSROOMS. THEN WE BOUGHT SOME PENCILS AT SCHIRMER'S MUSIC STORE DOWNSTAIRS. THEN WE EXAMINED THE BULLETIN BOARDS.

UNFORTUNATELY, ALL OF THIS ONLY TOOK ABOUT TEN MINUTES. BUT THE DIVERSION WAS WORKING. I HAD NOT THROWN UP, AND I WAS BLINKING MUCH MORE SLOWLY.

TELL YOU WHAT, MARVIN. LET'S GO UP ON THE *ROOF*. IT'S A BEAUTIFUL DAY!

IT SEEMED LIKE A GREAT IDEA. I HAD WOLFED DOWN A HANDFUL OF MAALOX TABLETS AND FELT PRETTY GOOD...

FATHER AND SON STROLLING ON THE ROOF— WHAT COULD BE NICER?

WE TOOK IN THE GLORIES OF NEW YORK, LOOKING ACROSS THE BUILDINGS AT *GRANT'S TOMB*, WHICH STOOD NEARBY.

I COULDN'T HELP WONDERING IF GRANT'S TOMB WAS THE FINAL RESTING PLACE...

...OF SOME JUILLIARD STUDENT NAMED *"GRANT"* WHO FAILED THE EXAM.

BACK CAME THE NERVES. MY FATHER QUIETED ME DOWN, AND WE STARTED TO TALK.

FINALLY, I GOT BRAVE ENOUGH TO ASK:

DADDY, WHY DO I HAVE TO GO TO JUILLIARD?

MARVIN, I KNOW THIS IS HARD FOR YOU, BUT YOU CAN'T GIVE UP. GOD GAVE YOU A TALENT — YOU MUSTN'T WASTE IT.

I *KNOW* YOU CAN DO IT!

HE TOLD ME OVER AND OVER THAT I HAD BEEN GIVEN THIS GIFT AND THAT TO WASTE IT WOULD LET DOWN GOD, MY PARENTS, AND MYSELF.

I BEGAN TO UNDERSTAND WHY, FOR HIM, IT WAS SO IMPORTANT FOR ME TO STICK WITH THIS.

UNLIKE MY FATHER, I WASN'T GOING TO BE DRIVEN OUT OF MY HOMELAND.

"GOD HAS NOT JUST GIVEN YOU YOUR TALENT, MARVIN," HE SAID. "HE'S PUT YOU IN A LAND WHERE YOU KNOW THE LANGUAGE, A PLACE WHERE NO ONE CAN TAKE SUCCESS AWAY FROM YOU."
I NODDED. "MARVIN, YOU ARE PROBABLY TOO YOUNG TO UNDERSTAND THIS. WHAT I'M GIVING YOU IS A RARE THING. I NEVER HAD THE CHANCE MYSELF. HERE IN THIS BUILDING THERE'S A FOUNDATION YOU'RE GETTING THAT WILL STAY WITH YOU *FOREVER*. MUSICAL TRAINING HAS TO START YOUNG. IT HAS TO GET INTO YOUR BLOOD. OVER AND OVER AND OVER, PRACTICE, PRACTICE, PRACTICE, MARVIN," HE SAID LOVINGLY.

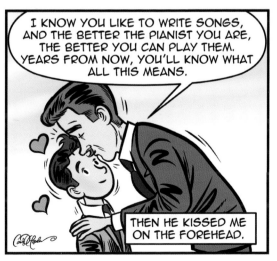

I KNOW YOU LIKE TO WRITE SONGS, AND THE BETTER THE PIANIST YOU ARE, THE BETTER YOU CAN PLAY THEM. YEARS FROM NOW, YOU'LL KNOW WHAT ALL THIS MEANS.

THEN HE KISSED ME ON THE FOREHEAD.

I LOOKED DOWN AT MY WATCH. THERE WERE ONLY *FIVE MINUTES* TO GO.

THE TALK WITH MY FATHER HAD CALMED ME DOWN. I FELT FINE. I COULD FACE THE JURY AND PLAY MY BEST. I HAD NOT THROWN UP. I WAS IN COMMAND. I WAS READY.

WE HEADED FOR THE DOOR TO THE ROOF. IT WAS *LOCKED*.

KLUNK!

CLICK! CLACK!

INSTANT HYSTERIA!

THE JURY WAITED BELOW AND I WAS UP ON THE ROOF, STRUGGLING WITH A LOCKED IRON DOOR!

CLANG! CLANG!

NOOO!

WE RAN TO THE EDGE OF THE ROOF, LEANED FAR OVER THE EDGE, AND STARTED TO SHOUT AT THE TOP OF OUR LUNGS

HELP! HELP!

I WAS PERSPIRING INTO MY NEW WOOLEN SUIT, AND FATHER AND SON WERE OVERCOME BY PANIC.

FINALLY, WE ATTRACTED SOMEBODY'S ATTENTION ON THE STREET...

AND AFTER ENOUGH TIME TO TURN A CONFIDENT STUDENT INTO A RAVING *MANIAC*...

KLANK!

THE SUPERINTENDENT ARRIVED TO OPEN THE DOOR.

WHEN I REACHED THE JURY TWENTY-FIVE MINUTES LATE, I WAS A PATHETIC SIGHT. MY NERVES WERE SHOT.

I HANDED THE THREE TYPEWRITTEN, NOW SLIGHTLY WRINKLED SHEETS TO THE JURORS.

AFTER I PLAYED A FEW SCALES, THEY ASKED ME TO PLAY SOME OF THE KABALEVSKY. BUT AS I RAISED MY FINGERS ABOVE THE KEYBOARD, I HEARD A TITTER FROM ONE OF THE JURORS.

HAHA!

GIGGLE!

THEN I HEARD A LAUGH FROM ANOTHER.

I WAS CONCENTRATING WITH ALL MY MIGHT ON THE SONATA, AND AS I HAD BEEN TAUGHT, I KEPT MY EYES ON THE KEYS.

HA! HA! HA!

BUT AS I LOOKED DOWN, I SAW THE LITTLE ORANGE BEARS AND INDIANS PEEKING OUT OF THE CUFFS OF MY PANTS, STARING UP AT ME.

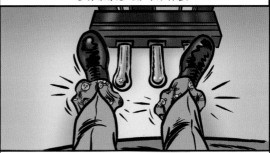

WELL, I PASSED THE DREADED ANNUAL EXAM AND WON THE RIGHT TO DO IT AGAIN NEXT YEAR. I LOVE HAPPY ENDINGS.

I AM A GREAT BELIEVER IN THE JURY SYSTEM, BUT NOT FOR SIX-YEAR-OLDS.

POLIO VACCINE VOLUNT

MY PARENTS VIEWED THE STRESS OF THOSE EXAMS AS THEY VIEWED A POLIO SHOT— AS NECESSARY AND *TRANSITORY* DISCOMFORT.

LOOKING BACK ON THOSE EARLY DAYS OF PAIN AND PANIC, I REALLY DON'T BELIEVE THAT THE MIND OF A YOUNG CHILD IS DESIGNED TO HANDLE THIS KIND OF PRESSURE. AT SUCH AN EARLY AGE YOU ARE ALREADY AUDITIONING. YET, YOU MIGHT NOT BELIEVE THIS, BUT IF I HAD TO DO IT AGAIN, I WOULD. I'D DO IT FOR THOSE *FIFTY MINUTES* ON THE ROOF, *ALONE WITH MY FATHER.*

THE EXAMINATION WAS HELL, BUT *THOSE FIFTY MINUTES WITH MAX HAMLISCH WERE SHEER HEAVEN.*

I HAVE SPENT MORE TIME WITH THE PIANO THAN WITH ANYBODY. I HAVE ALWAYS FELT COMFORTABLE AROUND IT, AND IT SEEMS LIKE MY OLDEST FRIEND.

IT'S ONE REASON WHY I CAN GIVE A CONCERT IN ONE CITY, FLY TO ANOTHER, AND FEEL PERFECTLY AT HOME WHEN I STEP ONSTAGE. BECAUSE THERE IT IS, MY OLD BUDDY, THE PIANO. A PIANO CAN BE A *PROTECTIVE ARMOR* AGAINST THE WORLD.

EVEN IN FIRST GRADE AT P.S. 9 ON 82ND STREET AND BROADWAY, I WAS THE TYPE OF KID WITH A PERPETUAL NERVOUS STOMACH, FRIGHTENED TO BE ALONE, AND CONSTANTLY NEEDING SOMEONE TO CLING TO.

Welcome to P.S. 9

MY FATHER WAS BUSY TRYING TO MAKE A LIVING WITH HIS ACCORDION, SO MY MOTHER WAS ELECTED TO BE MY UBIQUITOUS PROTECTOR AND CONFIDANTE.

IN THOSE DAYS MY FATHER SOUGHT JOBS AT A MYSTERIOUS PLACE CALLED "THE UNION," A MEETING HALL FOR MEMBERS OF MUSICIANS UNION 802.

LOCAL 802

HE USUALLY DID THIS IN THE AFTERNOON, WORKED AT NIGHT, AND CAME HOME IN THE EARLY HOURS OF THE MORNING.

THEREFORE, I SAW HIM MOSTLY ON WEEKENDS AND AT DINNERTIME. I SAW A LOT MORE OF MY MOTHER – THE INSTANT I AWOKE...

HOPALONG CASSIDY

MARVIN

...AND WHEN I RETURNED FROM SCHOOL AT THREE O'CLOCK.

IN FIRST GRADE I HAD A TEACHER NAMED MISS MORRISON WHO I REMEMBER AS A CROSS BETWEEN EVA BRAUN AND THE WICKED WITCH OF THE WEST. SHE MADE ME *VERY NERVOUS.*

Hello my name is MISS MORRISON

I HAD LITTLE STOMACH FOR BREAKFAST, SO MY MOTHER WOULD GIVE ME A PACKET OF SOCIAL TEA BISCUITS TO EAT AT THE ELEVEN O'CLOCK MILK BREAK.

Social Tea

BUT WHEN YOU'VE SKIPPED BREAKFAST YOUR APPETITE COMES EARLY. TO THIS DAY, FRIENDS KNOW THAT WHEN I GET HUNGRY, MY WHOLE PERSONALITY CHANGES.

I FELT FAINT AND FURIOUS. LIKE AN ADDICT, I DOVE FOR THE ONLY THING THAT COULD SATISFY MY CRAVINGS. I NEEDED THOSE *COOKIES!*

MARVIN, YOU CANNOT EAT BEFORE THE REST OF THE CLASS. YOU WILL HAVE TO WAIT TILL ELEVEN!

SHE MADE IT SOUND LIKE THE ELEVENTH COMMANDMENT. SO I *KICKED* HER.

CLOP!

YOU HEARD ME, I KICKED MISS MORRISON VERY HARD IN THE ANKLE, RIGHT THROUGH HER ORTHOPEDIC STOCKINGS

I COULD SEE THE HEADLINES IN THE *NEW YORK TIMES*:

I KNEW THIS WOULD BE AN ENORMOUS EMBARRASSMENT TO MY PARENTS, PARTICULARLY MY FATHER.

WE MIGHT HAVE BEEN LIVING IN NEW YORK, BUT HIS VALUES WERE PURE VIENNA, AND THE IDEA OF ASSAULTING SOMEONE WHO WAS GIVING YOU AN EDUCATION, WELL, THAT WAS UNTHINKABLE. NO SOONER DID I COMMIT MY HEINOUS CRIME THAN, HORRIFIED BY MY DEED AND ITS IMPLICATIONS, I RACED HOME AND TOLD MY MOTHER WHAT I HAD DONE. SHE WAS LOVING AND SUPPORTIVE AS USUAL. "DON'T WORRY, EVERYTHING WILL BE ALL RIGHT. I KNOW YOU MUST FEEL VERY SORRY. RIGHT NOW IT SEEMS LIKE A TERRIBLE THING. BUT YOU'LL HAVE A NICE GLASS OF MILK..."

AND THEN, WHEN YOUR FATHER GETS HOME...

HE'LL *KILL* YOU!

MY MOTHER DIDN'T HAVE TO TELL ME. SO, FILLED WITH CONTRITION AND FEAR, I DID THE PRUDENT, SENSIBLE, LOGICAL THING. I HID IN A SUITCASE.

SINCE THE SUITCASE WAS SMACK IN THE MIDDLE OF THE LIVING-ROOM FLOOR, MY FATHER FOUND ME. IT DIDN'T TAKE HIM LONG.

FIRST HE LOOKED IN THE CLOSET, THEN IN THE PIANO, THEN IN THE SUITCASE. BINGO.

WHEN MY FATHER HEARD THAT I HAD KICKED MY TEACHER, SOMETHING SNAPPED. I HAD DONE SOMETHING *UNPARDON-ABLE*, AND NOW HE DID SOMETHING THAT FOR HIM *WAS UNTHINKABLE.*

HE ONLY HIT ME ONCE IN MY LIFE, AND THIS WAS IT. I STILL REMEMBER THAT MOMENT. IT WAS A TERRIBLE SHOCK.

MY MOTHER DEALT WITH THE PROBLEM IN A TOTALLY DIFFERENT WAY.

SHE REALIZED THAT MY FRUSTRATION LAY IN MY BEING TERRIBLY HUNGRY AND BEING NERVOUS AT LEAVING HER SIDE. I HAD COPED WITH KINDERGARTEN, ALL RIGHT, BUT MISS MORRISON WAS A WHOLE NEW BALL GAME.

MY MOTHER DECIDED I NEEDED TO BE WEANED AWAY FROM HER APRON STRINGS RATHER THAN GOING COLD TURKEY INTO MISS MORRISON'S CLUTCHES EACH MORNING, SO FROM THEN ON, SHE STARTED COMING TO SCHOOL WITH ME EVERY DAY— AND STAYING.

SHE WOULD BRING ME TO P.S. 9 EACH MORNING, AND THEN, UNDAUNTED, SETTLE INTO A CHAIR IN THE CORRIDOR OUTSIDE THE CLASSROOM.

NO MATTER WHAT MISS MORRISON WOULD DO OR SAY TO ME, I WOULD HAVE THE COMFORTING KNOWLEDGE THAT MY MOTHER WAS NEARBY.

IN FACT, WHENEVER I FELT THE LEAST BIT INSECURE, I WAS ALLOWED TO LEAVE MY LITTLE SEAT, LOOK OUT THE DOOR, AND SATISFY MYSELF THAT SHE WAS STILL OUT THERE.

MY MOTHER'S VIGIL CONTINUED FOR THREE MONTHS, AND DURING THE LAST MONTH IT SLOWLY MELTED AWAY. HER SENTRY DUTY WAS FIRST CUT TO THREE HOURS A DAY, THEN NINETY MINUTES, THEN AN HOUR, AND FINALLY, SHE WASN'T OUT THERE ANYMORE.
BUT I HAD KICKED MISS MORRISON, AND THE BOARD OF EDUCATION OF THE CITY OF NEW YORK HAD NEITHER FORGIVEN NOR FORGOTTEN.

THE SCHOOL HAD LABELED ME *A TRUANT*, AND MY PARENTS RECEIVED A SOLEMN LETTER TO THAT EFFECT.

MY FUTURE WAS HOPELESSLY TAINTED – SIX YEARS OLD AND REPORTING TO A GUIDANCE COUNSELOR. NEXT STOP: THE PAROLE BOARD.

DESPITE THE TERROR OF WHAT AWAITED ME, THE GUIDANCE COUNSELOR TURNED OUT TO BE A TERRIFIC GUY. HE GAVE ME INTERESTING THINGS TO DO...

...LIKE LETTING ME PLAY WITH HIS STOPWATCH. THAT I LOVED. TO ME HE WAS "THE STOPWATCH DOCTOR."

ANY STUDENTS OF IRONY WILL WANT TO NOTE THAT TWENTY-FIVE YEARS LATER, A STOPWATCH WOULD BECOME MY BASIC TOOL IN SCORING HOLLYWOOD MOVIES.

MY FATHER, SEEING THE PLEASURE THE STOPWATCH GAVE ME...

...PROMPTLY BOUGHT ME MY OWN SO I COULD PLAY WITH IT AT HOME.

MEANWHILE, WE CONCLUDED OUR SESSIONS AND I WAS RETURNED TO A PRODUCTIVE LIFE IN THE CLASSROOM, A TRUANT NO MORE.

HE EVEN RECOMMENDED THAT I BE ALLOWED TO EAT SOME COOKIES IN CLASS IF I WAS HUNGRY.*

MUNCH! MUNCH!

DR. STOPWATCH HAD SAID, IN EFFECT, "GIVE THIS BOY A PIANO," AND THEY DID.

AN OLD UPRIGHT MATERIALIZED IN MY CLASSROOM.

*TO THIS DAY, THERAPISTS CALL THIS THE DUNCAN HINES THEORY OF CHILD PSYCHOLOGY.

MY FRIEND THE PIANO AND I WERE NEVER GOING TO BE SEPARATED AGAIN.

WHEN THE SECOND GRADE BEGAN, THE UPRIGHT WAS MOVED INTO MY NEW CLASSROOM.

MISS MORRISON WAS GONE, AND MY NEW TEACHER WAS *MISS SUSSMAN*.

BY THE TIME I REACHED THE SIXTH GRADE, I WAS PLAYING THE PIANO RATHER WELL. I NOT ONLY PLAYED THE PIECES I WAS TAUGHT BY MY TEACHER AT JUILLIARD BUT I...

...COULD PLAY MOST SONGS I HEARD ON THE RADIO "BY EAR"! I ALSO HAD PERFECT PITCH.

YOU MAY WONDER WHAT IT'S LIKE TO HAVE PERFECT PITCH AND A GOOD EAR. I'VE ALWAYS WONDERED WHAT IT'S LIKE *WITHOUT THEM.*

I MEAN, I'M ONE OF THE FEW PEOPLE WHO GOES TO A MOVIE AND HEARS THE MUSIC INSTEAD OF THE DIALOGUE.

MY FIRST PARLOR PERFORMANCE CAME AT THE REQUEST OF MY BELOVED MISS SUSSMAN.

SHE PROPOSED TO HIRE ME TO PLAY AT A PARTY SHE WAS GIVING AT HER HOME FOR SOME TEACHER FRIENDS.

THE SCHOOL YEAR WAS NEARLY OVER, THE DREADED JUILLIARD EXAM BEHIND ME, AND THE WEATHER WAS SUNNY AND WARM.

SO THE DAY BEFORE THE PARTY, I DONNED SOME RAGGED BLUE JEANS AND WENT OUTSIDE TO DO WHAT I LOVED TO DO— PLAY BALL.

IN CASE YOU MISSED THE CHANCE TO GROW UP ON THE STREETS OF MANHATTAN, I SHOULD POINT OUT THE SOCIO-LOGICAL ODDITY THAT NEW YORK CITY STREETS ARE ACTUALLY BALL FIELDS. ON WEST 81ST STREET BETWEEN COLUMBUS AND AMSTERDAM AVENUES, THE LAMPPOST SERVES AS FIRST BASE, THE SEWER MANHOLE IS SECOND, THE CHURCH STEPS ARE THIRD, AND WHEREVER YOU WANT IS HOME. NOW, IN THIS PICKUP GAME OF BASE-BALL, I WAS THE *CATCHER*.

THIS WAS A SINGULARLY HAZARDOUS POSITION. YOU WILL NEVER SEE A PHOTOGRAPH OF LEONARD BERNSTEIN PLAYING CATCHER, AND THERE'S A VERY GOOD REASON, WHICH I WAS ABOUT TO LEARN.

IF THE TRAJECTORY OF THIS SWING HAD BEEN A HALF INCH LOWER, I WOULD NOW BE STARRING IN PIRATE MOVIES.

TO THIS DAY, I CLEARLY REMEMBER THE LOOK OF PURE HORROR ON MY MOTHER'S FACE AND THE COOL, METHODICAL WAY SHE DEALT WITH CALAMITY.

THE NEXT DAY, I HAD A REAL SHINER. WHAT WAS UPPERMOST IN MY TEN-YEAR-OLD MIND, ONCE THE PAIN SUBSIDED...

...WAS THAT I DIDN'T WANT TO *LET MY TEACHER DOWN*.

AT THE APPOINTED HOUR I ENTERED THE SUSSMAN DOMICILE. MY EYE WAS A RHAPSODY IN PURPLE.

GOOD LORD, WHO HIT YOU?

I NEVER GOT THE CHANCE TO EXPLAIN. I PLAYED A MEDLEY OF POP AND BROADWAY MUSIC FOR THE APPRECIATIVE GUESTS.

A NEW CATEGORY FOR THE OSCARS: "BEST PERFORMANCE BY A CHILD PIANIST WITH A BLACK EYE."

HOW BRAVE!

SUCH COURAGE!

SO TALENTED!

OUR SIXTH-GRADE CLASS AT P.S. 9 PUT ON A PRODUCTION OF *H.M.S. PINAFORE*. I WAS IN CHARGE, AN ELEVEN-YEAR-OLD IMPRESARIO. I TAUGHT THE SONGS, REHEARSED THE CAST, SHORTENED CERTAIN PARTS, AND PLAYED THE MUSIC.

I GUESS YOU'D SAY THIS WAS MY FIRST EXPERIENCE WITH MOUNTING A SHOW, AND I LOVED IT. IT ALL CAME NATURALLY. IT WAS AT THIS TIME THAT THE YOUNG MAN WHO WOULD LATER MARRY MY SISTER BEGAN TO PLAY AN IMPORTANT ROLE IN MY LIFE.

HOWARD LIEBLING WAS MY MOTHER'S BROTHER'S WIFE'S BROTHER. GOT IT? HE BECAME MY FIRST LYRICIST,

AND SO THE TWENTY-SEVEN-YEAR-OLD HOWARD AND THE ELEVEN-YEAR-OLD MARVIN FORMED AN UNLIKELY COLLABORATION THAT WOULD SOON PRODUCE MORE THAN A FEW SONGS

IN OUR BATHROOM WE HAD A RADIO THAT I KEPT TUNED TO WABC, WHERE A DJ CALLED COUSIN BRUCIE REGULARLY PLAYED THE TOP-FORTY HITS.

THIS KEPT ME WIRED INTO THE SOUNDS OF THE DAY...

BUT IT HAD A STRANGE EFFECT ON MY COMPOSING. MY SONGS SOUNDED UNCANNILY LIKE WHATEVER I HEARD. IF ONE MORNING I HEARD A SONG CALLED "I LOVE YOU, BABY"

I WOULD WRITE A SONG CALLED *"I REALLY LOVE YOU, BABY."* I WAS THE ULTIMATE CHAMELEON COMPOSER.

WITH HOWARD AT MY SIDE, WE TURNED OUT DOZENS OF SONGS AND SPENT HOURS SCHEMING ABOUT HOW WE WOULD GET OUR *BIG BREAK.*

MY MOTHER CAME TO AMERICA FROM AUSTRIA, A CONSERVATIVE JEW. HER RELIGION WAS SACRED TO HER.

...SHE SECRETLY KEPT HER JEWISH STAR AROUND HER NECK, UNDER HER BLOUSE.

EVEN IN VIENNA, WHEN THE GESTAPO HAD HAULED HER IN FOR QUESTIONING...

SHE NEVER REMOVED IT.

MY FATHER WARNED HER: "LILLY, TAKE IT OFF. IT'S TOO DANGEROUS TO WEAR IN THE STREETS."

NO. *NEVER!*

FOUR HOLIDAYS WERE ESPECIALLY SIGNIFICANT IN OUR HOUSE: *PASSOVER, CHANUKAH, ROSH HASHANAH, AND YOM KIPPUR.*

THE LAST TWO WERE *SO MEANINGFUL* THAT WHEN MY MOTHER GOT A CALENDAR, SHE'D INSTANTLY CIRCLE THE DATES OF THESE TWO HOLIDAYS.

SEPTEMBER 1952

TO THIS DAY I DO THE SAME THING.

MY MOTHER AND FATHER WERE VERY DIFFERENT PEOPLE. HER FAVORITE SAYING WAS *"YOU'VE GOT TO MAKE ELBOWS,"* BY WHICH SHE MEANT: IN THIS BUSTLING WORLD OF SELF-ABSORBED PEOPLE, YOU HAVE TO MAKE YOURSELF A LITTLE ELBOW ROOM. MY FATHER, ON THE OTHER HAND, WAS MORE CAUTIOUS AND PESSIMISTIC. LET ME GIVE YOU AN EXAMPLE...MY SISTER AND I LOVED TO ATTEND THE MACY'S THANKSGIVING DAY PARADE.

OFTEN, THE HAMLISCH FAMILY, WHICH LIKED THEIR BEAUTY SLEEP, WAS LATE ARRIVING. ONCE, WHEN A POLICEMAN STANDING BY A WOODEN BARRIER BLOCKED OUR WAY, MY FATHER SHRUGGED...

YES, YES, I UNDERSTAND!

HE WAS READY TO TURN BACK. BUT MY MOTHER'S EYES WIDENED...

POLICE

MY MOTHER, LILLY SCHACHTER, WAS BORN IN VIENNA AND TRAINED AS A SEAMSTRESS. SHE LEFT SCHOOL AFTER THE THIRD GRADE BECAUSE HER MOTHER WAS ILL AND SHE HAD TO CARE FOR HER. LILLY WAS A BEAUTIFUL GIRL AND THE TARGET OF EVERY ELIGIBLE MALE IN THE INNER CITY. ONE OF THESE WAS A HANDSOME, WEALTHY YOUNG FELLOW WITH THE MUSICAL-COMEDY NAME OF *ERNST PICKHOLTZ.*

MY MOTHER'S FAMILY WAS ALL FOR HER MARRYING ERNST IMMEDIATELY BECAUSE, WITH THE CLOUDS OF NAZISM APPROACHING AUSTRIA, ERNST COULD WHISK HER OFF TO ARGENTINA.

IF HE HAD, SHE WOULDN'T HAVE HAD TO ESCAPE THE STORMTROOPERS IN THE PRECARIOUS WAY SHE DID...

...AND TODAY I WOULD BE *MARVIN PICKHOLTZ*...

...*COMPOSER OF EVITA!*

THE ONLY DOWNSIDE TO ERNST PICKHOLTZ WAS THAT MY MOTHER WAS ALREADY IN LOVE WITH ANOTHER MAN, A MUSICIAN NAMED *MAX HAMLISCH.*

BUT HE LACKED THE FINANCIAL MEANS TO GET HER OUT OF VIENNA. IT WAS THE OLD STORY OF A WOMAN CHOOSING BETWEEN *LOVE* AND *BUENOS AIRES.*

MY FATHER HAD STUDIED TO BE A COMMERCIAL ARTIST, BUT HIS FIRST LOVE WAS MUSIC, AND HE BARELY SCRAPED BY PLAYING AT DANCES.

HE MARRIED MY MOTHER AND THEY MOVED INTO A SMALL APARTMENT. THEY WOULD HAVE REMAINED THERE AND LIVED HAPPILY EVER AFTER, "THE BLUE DANUBE WALTZ" FOR UNDERSCORING, EXCEPT FOR ADOLF HITLER.

BY 1935, MAX KNEW IN HIS BONES, IT WAS TIME TO GO.

HITLER WAS NOT JUST A CHARLIE CHAPLIN LOOK-ALIKE – DER FÜHRER HAD AN APPETITE FOR CONQUEST, AND AUSTRIA WAS HIGH ON HIS MENU.

ONE DAY, A MUSICIAN FRIEND TOLD MY FATHER OF A JOB THAT WAS AVAILABLE IN THE WALD HOTEL IN THE TOWN OF VADUZ, ACROSS THE BORDER IN LIECHTENSTEIN.

THIS WAS THE POSTAGE-STAMP-SIZED COUNTRY IMMORTALIZED BY IRVING BERLIN IN *CALL ME MADAM.*

MY FATHER WAS ALLOWED TO COMMUTE BY TRAIN, AND HE CARRIED PAPERS THAT WERE STAMPED *HEIL HITLER.*

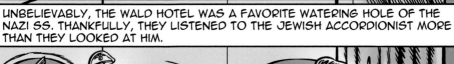

UNBELIEVABLY, THE WALD HOTEL WAS A FAVORITE WATERING HOLE OF THE NAZI SS. THANKFULLY, THEY LISTENED TO THE JEWISH ACCORDIONIST MORE THAN THEY LOOKED AT HIM.

THIS JOB WAS TO BECOME THE STEPPING-STONE FOR MY PARENTS' ESCAPE FROM AUSTRIA. ONLY MY FATHER HAD OFFICIAL PAPERS; MY MOTHER DIDN'T.

IN ORDER TO GET THEM, SHE HAD TO PRESENT HERSELF AT AN OFFICE AND WAIT IN A LINE, *FOR JEWS ONLY*, AND IN THESE GHOULISH TIMES, THAT HAD ITS DANGERS.

BUT MY MOTHER MADE ELBOWS. WITH GUTS AND NERVE SHE PUT HERSELF IN THE LINE FOR ARYANS.

BUT IT WAS TO NO AVAIL. THE LINE WAS ENDLESS, AND THERE WERE NO DOCUMENTS TO BE HAD.

SO EACH DAY MY FATHER COMMUTED TO HIS JOB BY TRAIN, AND EACH DAY THE PRESSURES ON AUSTRIAN JEWS CONTINUED TO BUILD.

MY PARENTS' ESCAPE FROM AUSTRIA WAS COMPLETELY SERENDIPITOUS. ON THE TRAIN MY FATHER CARRIED ALL HIS INSTRUMENTS WITH HIM.

MY MOTHER PACKED A SMALL SUITCASE FOR HIM EACH NIGHT. PACKING WAS ONE OF THE THINGS SHE DID BETTER THAN ANY LIVING PERSON.

EVERY EVENING HE TRAVELED BACK AND FORTH WITH A FLUTE, A CLARINET, A SAXOPHONE, AND AN ACCORDION. HE OFTEN PLAYED FOR THE OTHER PASSENGERS AND WAS SOON ACCEPTED AS ONE OF THE COMMUTING REGULARS.

SHE HAD THE ABILITY TO CRAM THREE SUITCASES WORTH OF THINGS INTO ONE. NO CUBIC INCH WENT UNUSED.

TOOTHBRUSHES SLID INTO SHIRT POCKETS, AND ALARM CLOCKS WENT INTO SLIPPERS ALONG WITH SOCKS AND UNDERWEAR.

NO SUITCASE WAS COMPLETE UNLESS IT CONTAINED SOME FRUIT. BECAUSE MY FATHER LOVED GRAPEFRUIT, MY MOTHER ALWAYS PACKED A BIG ONE FOR HIM.

PLOP!

HER SOLUTION IN THIS CASE WAS TO RAM IT INTO THIS SAXOPHONE.

ONE NIGHT ON THE TRAIN, THE CONDUCTOR WARNED MY FATHER.

MAX, THIS TRAIN IS *NOT GOING* TO LIECHTENSTEIN.

WE'VE BEEN REROUTED TO GERMANY. THEY'RE STARTING TO ARREST JEWS.

WHEN THE TRAIN STARTS TO SLOW DOWN, THAT'S THE SIGNAL: THAT'S THE *TIME TO JUMP!*

THAT NIGHT, AN OFFICIOUS YOUNG AUSTRIAN OFFICER ASKED TO SEE EVERYONE'S PAPERS. HE STRODE INTO EACH COMPARTMENT AND DEMANDED THAT JEWISH PASSENGERS COME FORWARD.

WHEN HE REACHED MY FATHER AND SAW THE SAXOPHONE CASE, HE GREW SUSPICIOUS.

MY FATHER SWORE IT WAS ONLY A MUSICAL INSTRUMENT, BUT THE YOUNG OFFICER WAS INTENT ON SHOWING HIS AUTHORITY.

OPEN IT AT ONCE!

FLIP!

GRAB!

THE OFFICER LOOKED HUMILIATED. NOT TO LET THE INCIDENT PASS, HE SEIZED THE INSTRUMENT, LIFTED IT OVER HIS HEAD, AND SHOOK IT.

HA! HA! HA! FLOP! HA! HA!

DERISIVE LAUGHTER IS NOT WELCOME TO YOUNG NAZIS. THE OFFICER HAD LOST FACE TO A JEW.

I KNOW YOU'RE LYING! YOU'RE HIDING SOMETHING!! TAKE OFF ALL YOUR CLOTHES! I'M GOING TO SEARCH YOU!

MY FATHER STARTED TO UNDRESS WHEN THE TRAIN SUDDENLY BEGAN TO SLOW DOWN.

THE OFFICER WENT TO SEE WHAT WAS HAPPENING; HE WAS GONE FOR ONLY A MINUTE...

... BUT THAT WAS ENOUGH!

WHEN HIS FRIENDS SAW HIM FLEEING THE TRAIN, THEY OPENED THE WINDOW AND THREW OUT HIS INSTRUMENTS.

HE GATHERED THEM UP AND, WITH HIS ARMS FULL, HURRIED AWAY. JUST THEN, A WOMAN APPEARED ON THE ROAD, PUSHING AN EMPTY BABY CARRIAGE. IF IT HAPPENED IN A MOVIE YOU'D MUTTER "HOW CONVENIENT." BUT THERE SHE WAS.

MY FATHER LOADED HIS INSTRUMENTS INTO THE BABY CARRIAGE, AND THE TWO WALKED OFF TOWARD LIECHTENSTEIN.

AFTER CHECKING INTO THE WALD HOTEL, HE REALIZED THAT HE WAS A FUGITIVE FROM THE AUSTRIAN AUTHORITIES.

HE SENT WORD TO MY MOTHER THAT HE COULD NEVER RETURN TO VIENNA. SHE WOULD HAVE TO JOIN HIM AND THEN THEY MUST TRY TO GET TO AMERICA.

THE PRESSURE GREW ON MY MOTHER TO MAKE A SPEEDY EXIT. THE OLD WORLD WAS RAPIDLY BEING REPLACED BY AN UGLY NEW ONE. TWO DAYS LATER, MY MOTHER FOUND HERSELF ON A LIST. THE SUPERINTENDENT OF HER BUILDING HAD DENOUNCED HER. THIS WAS VERY COMMON IN VIENNA AT THAT TIME. SHE KNEW IT WOULD NOT BE LONG BEFORE THE NAZI COLLABORATORS CAME TO HER APARTMENT TO TAKE *ANYTHING VALUABLE*. ALL SHE HAD WAS THE HOUSE MONEY. SHE WAS CERTAIN THEY WOULD SEARCH IN THE USUAL PLACES. SHE UNSCREWED THE LIGHT BULB IN THE BATHROOM FIXTURE AND STUFFED THE CASH INTO THE *SOCKET*.

ON THE DAY SHE WAS EVICTED, THE SUPERINTENDENT SEARCHED THE APARTMENT. THEN HE SEARCHED THE CLOTHES MY MOTHER WAS WEARING.

FINDING NOTHING, HE ORDERED HER TO LEAVE AT ONCE. ALL SHE WAS PERMITTED TO TAKE WAS AN OVERCOAT.

AS SHE WAS BEING ESCORTED TO THE STREET, SHE CONVINCED HIM SHE HAD TO GO BACK AND USE THE BATHROOM.

MY FATHER MADE ARRANGEMENTS TO SMUGGLE HER OUT OF AUSTRIA ON THE FLOOR OF A CAR, COVERED BY OVERCOATS.

A FEW WEEKS LATER, THEY LEFT LIECHTENSTEIN AND WERE GRANTED A TEMPORARY VISA IN SWITZERLAND.

MY MOTHER GOT A WONDERFUL JOB THERE, WORKING AT A DAYCARE CENTER FOR CHILDREN.

SHE WAS BORN TO BE AROUND CHILDREN; SHE HAD A GIFT THAT MADE HER CARING AND PATIENT WITH THEM.

HAD THEY BEEN PERMITTED, THEY WOULD HAVE STAYED IN SWITZERLAND AND I WOULD HAVE SPENT MY DAYS IN A CHOCOLATE FACTORY.

TOOOT!

MY MOTHER HAD A BROTHER, ERNST, IN CHICAGO, AND SHE YEARNED TO BE WITH HIM. MY PARENTS' ROUTE TOOK THEM TO ITALY, AND THEY FINALLY SAILED FOR THE UNITED STATES.

THEY LANDED AT ELLIS ISLAND AND DISEMBARKED ON THANKSGIVING DAY, 1937.

IT WASN'T FOR SEVERAL DAYS THAT THEY REALIZED AMERICANS DO NOT EAT TURKEY AND CRANBERRY SAUCE EVERY DAY.

THE ORIGINAL PLAN WAS TO GO STRAIGHT TO CHICAGO, BUT WE ALSO HAD A RELATIVE IN NEW YORK – A MAN I CAME TO CALL MY "UNCLE SYRUP," BECAUSE HE HAD AMASSED A FORTUNE SELLING SWEET, FRUIT-FLAVORED SYRUP.

WHEN MY FATHER TOLD HIM OF HIS PLANS TO GO TO CHICAGO, MY SYRUP UNCLE TOOK HIM ASIDE...

MAX, STAY IN NEW YORK. IF YOU CAN MAKE IT *HERE*, YOU'LL MAKE IT *ANYWHERE!*

SLIP!

SO MY PARENTS BECAME *NEW YORKERS*.

IT WAS HARD TO LEARN THE NEW LANGUAGE AND ADJUST TO THE FAST PACE AND STYLE OF LIFE. WHERE WERE THE COURTLY MANNERS...

WAS IST DENN DAS??

...AND THE GENTLE MUSIC? MY FATHER COULD NOT FATHOM WHAT HE HEARD ON THE RADIO.

MY FATHER WAS VERY TALENTED, AND HAD HE BEEN ALLOWED TO STAY IN HIS HOMELAND, PERHAPS HE WOULD HAVE BEEN ABLE TO REACH HIS TRUE POTENTIAL.

WALDORF ASTORIA

INSTEAD, HE WOULD HAVE TO LIVE OUT HIS LIFE, YEAR AFTER YEAR, PLAYING VIENNESE BALLS.

YET HE COULD NEVER REALLY FEEL COMFORTABLE IN AMERICA. HE KNEW HE WAS NOT STRETCHING HIS MUSICAL HORIZONS IN NEW YORK, AND PERHAPS THAT INNER STRUGGLE LED HIM TO ATTACH HIS THWARTED HOPES ONTO HIS SON. BUT THOSE ABORTED DESIRES NEVER LEFT HIM, AND I THINK THEY CHEWED AT HIM FOR THE REST OF HIS LIFE. ALL MY MOTHER WANTED, WHEN THEY GOT HERE, WAS TO START A FAMILY. HE WAS DEAD SET AGAINST THE IDEA.

THERE'S NO MONEY, LILLY! BIST DU *VERRÜCKT?*

ON SEPTEMBER 2, 1943, A COOL, BREEZY AUTUMN EVENING, LILLY MADE ONE OF HER RENOWNED DINNERS, A *SPECIAL TREAT* TO END ALL TREATS. MY FATHER SNIFFED THE AIR AND KNEW THAT HE WAS ABOUT TO PARTAKE IN A MEAL UNLIKE ANY HE HAD EVER HAD.

BY EVENING'S END, MAX REACHED TOWARD HIS BELOVED AND WHISPERED, "LILLY, YOU'VE DONE SO MUCH FOR ME ALL THESE YEARS, HOW CAN I *EVER* REPAY YOU?" EXACTLY NINE MONTHS TO THE DAY, MARVIN HAMLISCH WAS BORN.

BY THE TIME I HAD COMPLETED THE SIXTH GRADE, I STARTED GOING TO BROADWAY SHOWS BY MYSELF. I HAD ALREADY SEEN AND LOVED THE *PAJAMA GAME*, *DAMN YANKEES*, AND *WEST SIDE STORY*. I STILL RECALL THE THRILL I GOT FROM HEARING JOHN RAITT SING "HEY THERE" IN TO A DICTAPHONE AND THEN SING A DUET WITH HIMSELF ON THE PLAYBACK. IT WAS SUCH A THEATRICAL MOMENT. SEEING GWEN VERDON DO "WHATEVER LOLA WANTS, LOLA GETS" IN *DAMN YANKEES* AND HEARING LARRY KERT SING "MARIA" MADE IT CLEAR THAT THIS WAS THE WORLD I WANTED TO LIVE IN.

IT WAS TIME TO ENROLL IN A JUNIOR HIGH SCHOOL. I WAS GOING TO JUILLIARD ON SATURDAYS, TAKING PIANO LESSONS, AND PRACTICING TWO HOURS A DAY. MY PARENTS THOUGHT I SHOULD ATTEND A SCHOOL THAT MADE *MINIMUM DEMANDS* ON MY TIME.

PROFESSIONAL CHILDREN'S SCHOOL

AFTER CHECKING THE PROFESSIONAL CHILDREN'S SCHOOL (PCS) AND ASSESSING THE ALTERNATIVES, MY FATHER DECIDED IT WAS THE PLACE FOR ME.

UNBEKNOWNST TO MY FATHER, HE WAS FEEDING MY LOVE OF SHOW BUSINESS. HE HAD PUT A RABBIT IN CHARGE OF THE LETTUCE.

THE STUDENT BODY OF PCS CONSISTED OF A HANDFUL OF ASPIRING, SERIOUS MUSICIANS BUT MAINLY OF KIDS WITH JOBS ON BROADWAY, IN THE MOVIES, ON TELEVISION, IN COMMERCIALS, IN MODELING. THESE WERE YOUNGSTERS MAKING MONEY, BUILDING CAREERS IN THE ENTERTAINMENT BUSINESS, AND GETTING THEIR EDUCATION AT THE SAME TIME.

PCS WAS THE PLACE WHERE, WHEN YOU ASKED A FELLOW STUDENT HOW HE OR SHE WAS DOING, THEY WOULD ANSWER:

ASK MY AGENT!

THERE WAS A PROBLEM WITH ALL THIS EXPOSURE TO BEAUTIFUL FACES AND BODIES. I BECAME PREOCCUPIED AND DISSATISFIED WITH HOW I LOOKED.

A COMPLEX TOOK ROOT AT PCS THAT WAS TO STAY WITH ME FOR A LONG TIME. I MEAN, *CHRISTOPHER WALKEN* WAS A CLASSMATE OF MINE!

THIS COMPLEX WAS QUITE PAINFUL FOR ME AT THE TIME, BUT MY PIANO ALWAYS CAME TO THE RESCUE. FOR WHEN I PLAYED IT, WATCH OUT— GIRLS SUDDENLY TOOK AN INTEREST IN ME.

WOW!

ANNA!

HEE. HEE!

I COULD COMPOSE A SONG ON THE SPOT USING *THEIR NAMES*.

IF NOTHING ELSE, PCS ACCELERATED MY APPETITE FOR MUSICALS. I WAS FINALLY MEETING THE KIDS WHO WERE OUT THERE DOING IT. THE GAP BETWEEN MY CLASSICAL MUSIC LESSONS AND MY POPULAR MUSIC LEANINGS GREW AS WIDE AS THE GRAND CANYON WHEN I GOT INVOLVED WITH CREATING SHOWS AT PCS THAT FEATURED THESE *REAL–LIVE PROFESSIONALS*.

BY THE TIME I REACHED THE NINTH GRADE, I MET A YOUNG FELLOW NAMED BOBBY MARIANO WHO PROMPTLY BECAME MY BEST FRIEND.

BOBBY WAS A DANCER APPEARING ON BROADWAY IN *THE MUSIC MAN*.

ONE DAY HE SAID TO ME:

WHY DON'T WE CREATE AN *ORIGINAL SCHOOL SHOW* AND STAGE IT IN A THEATER?

INSTANTLY, I FOUND MYSELF WRITING THE ENTIRE SCORE FOR A MUSICAL

I CALLED HOWARD LIEBLING TO WRITE THE SCORE, AND WE STARTED WORKING.

THE WAY I WORKED LATER IN MY CAREER HAS HARDLY CHANGED SINCE THOSE ROSY DAYS AT PCS. WHEN I THINK ABOUT A SONG, I START WITH WHAT IT SHOULD SAY, WHAT IT SHOULD *MEAN* IN THE SCENE THAT IT'S IN.

A FULL SET OF LYRICS, WITHOUT MUSIC, WOULD CONSTRAIN THE RHYTHM OF THE SONG. I LIKE TO WRITE THE MELODY FIRST. IF THE LYRICIST HANDS ME THE *FIRST FEW LINES*, THAT'S ENOUGH.

IT WAS 1960. WE MOUNTED IT IN A REAL THEATER, THE *LITTLE CARNEGIE*, WHICH NORMALLY SERVED AS A MOVIE HOUSE AND HAD AN HONEST-TO-GOD MARQUEE. ON OPENING NIGHT I HAD MY FIRST THRILL OF SITTING IN A THEATER AND HEARING A VOICE INSIDE ME SHOUT: "THEY'RE PLAYING MY SONG!" *"ALL OF US"* WAS A SMASH. IF NOTHING ELSE, IT WAS MY LAUNCHING-PAD EXPERIENCE. I MAY HAVE BEEN ONLY FIFTEEN, AND THE SHOW HAD ITS FAULTS FOR SURE, BUT I WAS ON MY WAY TO WRITING SOME PRETTY GOOD SONGS.

MEANWHILE, MY FRIEND BOBBY WAS DATING A GIRL CALLED *LIZA MINNELLI*. I KNEW SHE WAS VERY TALENTED EVEN THEN. THERE WERE NO BETTER VOCAL GENES THAN JUDY GARLAND'S AND NO BETTER THEATRICAL GENES THAN VINCENT MINNELLI'S. MOREOVER, LIZA HAD THOSE INCREDIBLE EYES AND TONS OF ENTHUSIASM.

THE THREE OF US— LIZA, BOBBY, AND I— SHARED SOME GREAT TIMES TOGETHER.

IT WAS CHRISTMAS OF 1960 WHEN LIZA CAME UP WITH AN INSPIRED IDEA FOR A GIFT FOR HER MOTHER. SHE WANTED TO RECORD SOME ORIGINAL SONGS AND GIVE THEM TO HER.

SHE WAS SO EXCITED ABOUT HOW THE DEMO SOUNDED THAT SHE INVITED BOBBY AND ME TO HER HOUSE FOR THE CHRISTMAS PARTY, DURING WHICH SHE WOULD PRESENT THE GIFT TO HER MOTHER.

"MARVIN," BOBBY SAID, "WHY DON'T YOU AND HOWARD WRITE SOME SONGS FOR LIZA?" HOWARD AND I PROMPTLY WROTE THEM; LIZA LOVED THEM AND RECORDED THE "DEMOS" IN A LITTLE STUDIO.

SIXTEEN-YEAR-OLD MARVIN HAMLISCH COULD HARDLY BELIEVE THAT HE WAS ABOUT TO MEET THE SINGER OF HIS DREAMS.

I WAS ALREADY AN ACCOMPLISHED COMPOSER WITH ONE HIGH SCHOOL PRODUCTION TO MY CREDIT. BUT MY COMPOSURE DESERTED ME THE INSTANT I ENTERED THE HOUSE.

I MEAN, I CAME FROM A TINY APART-MENT ON THE WEST SIDE OF MANHATTAN. THIS PLACE LOOKED LIKE THE PERFECT SETTING FOR THE SIGNING OF A *PEACE TREATY*.

THERE WERE WAITERS AND BUTLERS EVERYWHERE. NO ONE HAD EVER TOLD ME THAT HORS D'OEUVRES CAME BEFORE DINNER.

BUT MY MOTHER HAD TOLD ME TO MAKE SURE I WAS POLITE, AND SO I SAID YES TO EVERY PLATTER.

I WAS STUFFED AND WILDLY SURPRISED WHEN I HEARD:

DINNER IS SERVED!

AFTER WE'D FINISHED, IT WAS TIME TO EXCHANGE CHRISTMAS GIFTS. LIZA WENT OVER TO HER MOTHER AND HANDED HER A BEAUTIFULLY WRAPPED PACKAGE.

SHE ASKED FOR QUIET AS HER MOTHER OPENED IT. JUDY SEEMED STARTLED BY IT ALL.

LIZA TOOK THE RECORD FROM HER MOTHER. THERE WASN'T A SOUND IN THE HOUSE. THEN THE MUSIC STARTED, AND A VOICE FILLED THE ROOM. IT WAS A VOICE AT ONCE STRANGE AND FAMILIAR, YOUNG AND CONFIDENT.

AT FIRST, JUDY DIDN'T REALIZE WHO WAS SINGING. BUT WHEN SHE DID, SHE ACTUALLY WEPT. IT WAS ONE OF THE MOST STARTLING MOMENTS IN HER LIFE. AND I STOOD SPEECHLESS.

THEN JUDY CAME OVER TO ME, THANKED ME FOR WHAT I HAD DONE FOR LIZA, AND ASKED IN THAT GIRLISH VOICE OF HERS IF LIZA AND I WOULD DO IT AGAIN RIGHT THERE.

I WENT TO THE PIANO. LIZA SANG HER HEART OUT. IT WAS EVEN BETTER THAN THE DEMO.

BUT I WAS TOTALLY BOWLED OVER WHEN JUDY ASKED

WANNA PLAY FOR ME, MARVIN?

I NEVER THOUGHT I'D GET TO HEAVEN AT SIXTEEN, BUT I DID. I PLAYED THE PIANO AS JUDY GARLAND SANG "THE TROLLEY SONG" AND "SOMEWHERE OVER THE RAINBOW." IF I COULD HAVE PHONED THE WORLD THAT NIGHT, I WOULD HAVE. AS THE PARTY WOUND DOWN, JUDY ASKED IF I'D LIKE TO *SPEND THE NIGHT*. WHEN I HASTILY ACCEPTED, LIZA SHOWED ME TO A GUEST ROOM WITH A QUEEN-SIZED BED WITH BLUE SILK SHEETS AND BLUE SILK PILLOWCASES.

I WAS ENTHRALLED BY THE SILK SHEETS AND FLABBERGASTED BY THE FACT THAT I HAD MY OWN ROOM.

WHOA!

THERE WAS A PHONE BESIDE THE BED, AND I IMMEDIATELY USED IT.

"HELLO, MOM? YOU'RE NEVER GOING TO BELIEVE THIS. THEY LOVED THE RECORD AND THEN I PLAYED FOR JUDY GARLAND AND NOW I'M STAYING IN THE GUEST ROOM AND THERE ARE BLUE SILK SHEETS ON THIS REALLY HUGE BED AND BLUE SILK PILLOWCASES AND I DON'T HAVE TO SHARE THIS ROOM WITH ANYBODY."

"I PROBABLY WON'T GET UNDER THE COVERS BECAUSE I DON'T THINK I COULD MAKE THIS BED PROPERLY IN THE MORNING. I MEAN, THERE ARE TOP SHEETS AND SECOND SHEETS AND SHEETS FOR THE SHEETS..."

SO I SLEPT ON TOP OF THE COVERS WITH MY OVERCOAT AS A BLANKET.

WHEN IT WAS TIME TO LEAVE, I ASKED IF I COULD GET A LIFT TO THE TRAIN STATION. "THE TRAIN STATION?" JUDY ASKED. I WAS SENT HOME IN A CADILLAC LIMOUSINE. THE CAR WAS BIGGER THAN OUR LIVING ROOM. AS THE DRIVER TURNED ONTO WEST 81ST STREET, I WORRIED THAT THE CADDY MIGHT REBEL AT ITS ALIEN SURROUNDINGS. I MEAN, THIS WAS A SCARSDALE LIMOUSINE, AND HERE IT WAS IN THE GRIM, GRITTY CITY.

THAT NIGHT WHEN I WENT TO BED, MY MOTHER HAD GONE OUT AND USED HER POCKET MONEY TO BUY ME MY OWN BLUE SILK SHEETS.

MY JUDY GARLAND LIMOUSINE DAYS WERE SHORT-LIVED. I WAS BACK ON THE JAM-PACKED COLUMBUS AVENUE BUS ON THE WAY TO SCHOOL.

MY CLASSMATES WERE BUILDING WHIRLWIND CAREERS AND BREEZED IN AND OUT OF CLASS ONLY TO SEE THEIR AGENTS. NOTHING WOULD CONTAIN ME UNTIL THE RADIO IN THE BATHROOM WAS BLASTING MARVIN HAMLISCH. I CALLED UP HOWARD...

WHAT BEGAN AS A WEEKEND OF MUSICAL FRENZY GREW INTO MONTHS AND MONTHS OF TURNING OUT SONGS. WE HAD "PRETTY PENNY," "THEN YOU CAME ALONG," "EASTER SUNDAY," AND MORE... ON THE OPTIMISM SCALE OF ONE TO TEN, WE WERE BATTING ELEVEN. WE WERE ALREADY COUNTING THE MONEY.

WE WENT BACK TO THE RECORDING STUDIO AND MADE DEMOS. THIS TIME WE MADE UP OUR MINDS TO POUND THE PAVEMENTS, DOOR TO DOOR, AND FACE UP TO THESE RECORD GUYS. IN THE MUSIC BUSINESS, THERE WAS A NOTORIOUS LANDMARK CALLED THE BRILL BUILDING, WHERE NEW YORK'S MUSIC PUBLISHERS SUPPOSEDLY CONDUCTED THEIR BUSINESS.

YOU HAD TO ADMIRE THESE PEOPLE. IN AN OFFICE THE SIZE OF A BROOM CLOSET.

IT'S A *NO* FROM ME!

MUNCH! MUNCH!

THEY HAD TIME FOR LITTLE ELSE BUT TO TELL COMPOSERS THEY HATED THEIR MUSIC.

SOLLY PLOTKIN HAD NO USE FOR "PRETTY PENNY"; WE CAME OH, SO CLOSE WITH VINNY "DEBOSS" CINZA, WHO LISTENED TO ALL OF "I GOT YOUR TELEPHONE NUMBER FROM JOHNNY" BUT THEN SAID: "DON'T CALL ME, I'LL CALL YOU." AFTER MONTHS OF THESE TURNDOWNS, HOWARD AND I, UNFAZED, WENT BACK TO THE DRAWING BOARD. THIS TIME IT TOOK ONLY TWO DAYS TO STRIKE GOLD. TWO JEWISH BOYS CAME UP WITH A NOVELTY CHRISTMAS SONG: "WHAT DID YOU GET SANTA CLAUS FOR CHRISTMAS?"

THE NAME ON THE DOOR SAID *BIENSTOCK*. HE HAD THE CLEAR, HONEST EYES OF A USED-CAR SALES-MAN AND WAS PUFFING SMOKE IN MY FACE AS HE HALF-LISTENED TO THE CHRISTMAS SONG DEMO. WE WERE AT THE DOOR AND ON OUR WAY OUT...

HEY, KIDS, I LIKE THIS 'PRESENT FOR SANTA CLAUS' IDEA. I THINK I CAN *DO SOMETHING WITH IT.*

EACH DAY WHEN THE PHONE RANG, THERE WAS PANDEMONIUM.

"IT COULD BE MR. BIENSTOCK."

DRRRRING!!

IT MUST HAVE BEEN THE WEEK AFTER THANKS-GIVING, 1960 WHEN THE TELEPHONE RANG.

LILLY! CONGRATULATIONS!

MARVIN'S SONG IS ON THE RADIO. SOMETHING ABOUT A PRESENT FOR SANTA CLAUS.

AND NOW A SHORT WORD FROM SPONSORS

I FLEW TO THE RADIO, BUT I HAD MISSED IT. I COULDN'T HELP WONDERING WHY I HADN'T HEARD FROM MR. BIENSTOCK.

SLOWLY, SADLY, WE LEARNED ABOUT THAT FINE LINE BETWEEN PLAGIARISM AND COINCIDENCE. THE TRUTH WAS THAT THE SONG AUNT LOLLA HAD HEARD WAS NOT "WHAT DID YOU GET SANTA CLAUS FOR CHRISTMAS?" IT WAS "LET'S GIVE A CHRISTMAS PRESENT TO SANTA CLAUS." NOW, I GUESS IT'S POSSIBLE THAT SOME ONE ELSE COULD HAVE HAD OUR IDEA AT THE EXACT SAME TIME WE WROTE OUR ORIGINAL SONG. BUT BEING A JEWISH MOTHER, LILLY KNEW THAT HER SON'S SONG HAD BEEN "GESTOHLEN."

GRRRR!

I WAS DEVASTATED. I BEGAN TO REALIZE HOW VULNERABLE I WAS, HOW MUCH I WAS AT THE MERCY OF THE BIENSTOCKS OF THE WORLD. HOW MUCH OLDER WOULD I HAVE TO GET BEFORE SUCCESS WOULD BE MINE? SEVENTEEN? EIGHTEEN?

WHAT KIND OF A MUSICIAN DID I WANT TO BE, ANYWAY?

I REALIZED THAT MY MIND WAS LIKE A CASSETTE PLAYER.

WHEN THE MUSIC NEEDED TO BE IMPORTANT AND SERIOUS, CLICK... IT WAS TIME TO BE THE JUILLIARD PIANIST. IF I WAS WRITING A ROCK'N'ROLL TUNE, CLICK...

I SAW IT ALL BEFORE ME, LAID OUT LIKE A GIANT MAP. NOT ONLY WAS I GOING TO STICK IT OUT AT JUILLIARD, EVEN IF IT KILLED ME, BUT I WAS GOING TO WRITE THE NUMBER 1 HIT SONG BEFORE I WAS TWENTY-FIVE, WIN AN OSCAR BEFORE I WAS THIRTY, AND WRITE THE MUSIC FOR A SMASH BROADWAY SHOW BEFORE I WAS THIRTY-FIVE.

WHO WAS IT WHO SAID, "BE CAREFUL WHAT YOU WISH FOR; YOU MAY GET IT"?

HOWARD AND I HAD WRITTEN A POP SONG CALLED "SUNSHINE, LOLLIPOPS AND RAINBOWS." NOW COMES A BIT OF SERENDIPITY. *QUINCY JONES*, THEN HEAD OF MERCURY RECORDS, HAD AN APPOINTMENT TO SEE HIS EAR, NOSE, AND THROAT DOCTOR.

THE DOCTOR WAS LESTER COLEMAN, WHOM I HAD MET AT JUDY GARLAND'S PARTY. HE LIKED MY MUSIC AND HAD BECOME A LOBBYIST FOR MY TALENTS.

DR. COLEMAN DID A SIXTY-SECOND PITCH ON MY MUSICAL PROMISE.

QUINCY AGREED TO MEET WITH ME. A FEW WEEKS AFTER HE HEARD ME PLAY "SUNSHINE, LOLLIPOPS AND RAINBOWS," HE GOT PROFESSIONAL SINGER *LESLEY GORE* TO RECORD IT.

IN LESS THAN 2 MONTHS, IT SHOT TO NUMBER 4 ON THE CHARTS. MY PLAN WAS WORKING; I HAD MET THE CHALLENGE AND WON. WELL, SORT OF. I MEAN, WHEN THE SONG WAS PLAYED ON THE RADIO, THE DJ WOULD SAY: AND HERE COMES *LESLEY GORE'S BIG HIT...*

HOWARD AND I STRUCK AGAIN. AFTER THE SUCCESS OF "SUNSHINE, LOLLIPOPS AND RAINBOWS" ON THE CHARTS, WE CAME UP WITH A SONG CALLED "*CALIFORNIA NIGHTS*." LIKE "SUNSHINE," IT BECAME ANOTHER HIT FOR LESLEY GORE, RIDING TO NUMBER 3.

MY FATHER, THOUGH HE COULDN'T DENY MY ACHIEVEMENT, WAS CONVINCED MORE AND MORE THAT I WAS JUST WASTING MY TIME.

THAT'S NOT HOW I SAW IT AT ALL. WITH TWO SONGS ON THE CHARTS AND MONEY ROLLING IN, HOWARD AND I QUICKLY WROTE A THIRD SONG.

I ARRIVED AT THE PUBLISHER'S OFFICE, CERTAIN HE WAS EAGER TO HEAR THE NEW SONG FROM HIS HOT NEW TEAM. I WAS READY FOR THE ROYAL TREATMENT. SEATED IN HIS OUTER OFFICE, I WAITED FOR TEN MINUTES. THEN TWENTY. THEN *THIRTY*.

WHEN I WAS FINALLY SHOWN INTO HIS OFFICE, HE HAD KEPT ME WAITING FOR A TOTAL OF AN *HOUR AND THIRTY MINUTES*. THERE WAS NO APOLOGY. NOT A GRACE NOTE OF EXPLANATION.

SOMETHING INSIDE OF ME SNAPPED. NO, I DIDN'T KICK HIM IN THE SHIN AND HIDE IN A SUITCASE.

I'VE WRITTEN TWO HITS FOR YOU. I'VE MADE YOU A TON OF MONEY!!

THAT'S TRUE, MARVIN!

I WON'T BE TREATED LIKE THIS. YOU KNOW WHAT I'M GOING TO DO WITH THE SONG I BROUGHT YOU?

RRIIP! RRIP! RRIP!

AND I MARCHED OUT OF HIS OFFICE.

AS I RODE DOWN THE BRILL BUILDING ELEVATOR, I FELT AS IF I WERE CAUGHT IN A TRAP.

POP MUSIC WAS TAKING AN EMOTIONAL AND PHYSICAL TOLL. I STARTED GETTING STOMACH ACHES, BAD ONES. THIS COULD LEAD TO ULCERS.

I COULD BE STRICKEN AT THE VERY MOMENT WHEN THEATRICAL PRODUCER DAVID MERRICK WALKS INTO MY LIFE AND BEGS ME TO WRITE A SHOW.

PLEASE PLEASE! PLEEASE!

EVERY FRIDAY NIGHT, AS A CHILD AND STRETCHING FAR INTO ADULTHOOD, MY FAMILY AND I WENT TO SERVICES AT THE TEMPLE TWO BLOCKS FROM OUR APARTMENT. YALE GRADUATE COLE PORTER WAS FAMOUS AT MY TEMPLE; MARVIN HAMLISCH WAS A NAME TO CONTEND WITH. THIS WAS MEANINGFUL TO MY MOTHER, BECAUSE SHE WANTED TO HAND DOWN THIS FRIDAY TRADITION TO MY SISTER AND ME.

WHEN I WAS ABOUT SEVENTEEN YEARS OLD, I GOT AN 8:30 A.M. CALL ONE SATURDAY FROM MY RABBI.

MARVIN, YOU'VE GOT TO HELP US. YOU'VE GOT TO COME AND GET US THROUGH THE SERVICES THIS MORNING!!

THE *ORGANIST* IS *SICK!*

FADE UP ON THE MOUNT NEBOH TEMPLE. MARVIN SITS ASTRIDE THE MIGHTY ORGAN, LOOKING LIKE A TEENAGE *PHANTOM OF THE OPERA*.

MY PARENTS AND SISTER ARE SEATED UP FRONT, LOOKING ON WITH VISIBLE PRIDE WHILE I AM PUZZLING OVER WHICH KNOBS TO PULL TO MAKE THE ORGAN LOUD OR SOFT, VIBRATO OR TREMOLO.

DURING THE RESPONSIVE READING, WHEN RABBI AND CONGREGATION READ FROM ALTERNATE PASSAGES IN THE PRAYER BOOK, NO MUSIC WAS NEEDED. I SAT QUIETLY AND WAITED.

FINALLY, WE REACHED THE MOMENT FOR THE "SILENT DEVOTION." THE RABBI HAD EXPLAINED TO ME THAT THE MUSIC FOR THE SILENT DEVOTION MUST BE QUIET, CONTEMPLATIVE, INTENDED TO EASE THE SOUL. I FINGERED THE KEYS IN A SOLEMN WAY.

THEN I DECIDED TO MAKE MY MARK. AS THE CONGREGATION PRAYED AND MEDITATED, I WENT INTO A VERY SOMBER RENDITION OF...

SUNSHINE LOLLIPOPS AND RAINBOWS...

!!!

THE SERVICES FINALLY ENDED...

THANK YOU FOR HELPING US, MARVIN. I FOUND IT *VERY INSPIRATIONAL*, VERY *INSPIRING!*

I WANTED DESPERATELY TO WRITE THE NEXT GREAT AMERICAN MUSICAL. I WAS EIGHTEEN YEARS OLD AND REALLY READY, BUT NOBODY WAS GIVING ME THE CHANCE.

HOW WAS IT POSSIBLE THAT NOT A SINGLE THEATRICAL PRODUCER HAD THE INSIGHT, VISION, OR COURAGE TO RISK $800,000 ON A BRILLIANT, GIFTED, ADOLESCENT COMPOSER TO WRITE A BROADWAY MUSICAL?

AT ABOUT THIS TIME, LIZA MINNELLI GOT HER FIRST BIG BREAK: SHE WAS STARRING IN AN OFF-BROADWAY MUSICAL CALLED *BEST FOOT FORWARD*. IT ALSO STARRED GLENN (NOW CHRISTOPHER) WALKEN.

Best Foot Forward

AND THE PERSON WHO WAS TO BECOME MOST RELEVANT TO ME WAS THE MUSICAL DIRECTOR: BUSTER DAVIS.

JUST AS DR. COLEMAN HAD LOBBIED FOR ME WITH QUINCY JONES, LIZA HAD BEEN TELLING BUSTER ABOUT THIS GANGLY KID WHO WAS A SUPERMAN AT THE KEYBOARD. ONE DAY, SHE *INSISTED* THAT BUSTER SIMPLY *HAD TO* LET ME AUDITION FOR HIM.

I WAS A SHY, STRAITLACED BOY WHO WORE A NECKTIE TO SCHOOL. EVERY DAY, I'M SURROUNDED BY THESE VERY COOL KIDS WHILE I'M MUNCHING A TUNA FISH SANDWICH.

I SUDDENLY GET A PHONE CALL FROM BUSTER.

SWEETHEART, DARLING. LIZA SAYS YOU'RE TERRIFIC. LISTEN, CUTIE, I'M LOOKING FOR AN ASSISTANT ON A NEW SHOW I'M WORKING ON. COME PLAY FOR ME ON TUESDAY AT FOUR. LET'S DO IT AT MY APARTMENT, SWEETIE! BYEEE!

BUSTER'S APARTMENT WAS ON WEST FIFTY-EIGHTH STREET. BUSTER WAS WEARING DARK GLASSES. INDOORS.

WELCOME, SWEETIE!

SO, WHAT ARE YOU GOING TO PLAY?

THE OVERTURE FROM *GYPSY!*

HIT IT!

I PROCEED, POURING MY HEART INTO THE SCORE, PLAYING MY HEAD OFF. JUST AS I FINISHED...

BUSTER STARTED TALKING, AND IT SEEMED AS IF THERE'D BE NO END TO IT.

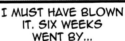

LOVED IT, SWEETIE! CALL YOU IN A COUPLE OF DAYS!

I WAS SURE I HAD PLAYED WELL, AND I HAD A FRIEND AT COURT IN *LIZA*. I WAS SO CONFIDENT, IN FACT, THAT I STRUCK A DEAL WITH MY FATHER. THE JOB WAS SCHEDULED TO BEGIN IN SEPTEMBER. THIS COINCIDED WITH MY FIRST SEMESTER AT COLLEGE. GRUDGINGLY, MY FATHER AGREED: I COULD TAKE ONE SEMESTER OFF FROM QUEENS COLLEGE IF I GAVE HIM MY *SOLEMN PLEDGE* TO RETURN TO SCHOOL— AFTER I FINISHED WITH THE SHOW— AND GET MY DEGREE. THAT WAS THE DEAL. I GRABBED IT. TWO OR THREE WEEKS WENT BY, AND I HEARD NOTHING. NOT A WHISPER.

I MUST HAVE BLOWN IT. SIX WEEKS WENT BY...

THEN EIGHT. WHERE WAS BUSTER?

I FINALLY MUSTERED THE COURAGE TO PHONE HIM.

DIDN'T YOU LIKE MY PLAYING? WHY DON'T I HAVE THE JOB?

MARVIN, YOU WERE *FABULOUS!* THE SHOW'S BEEN POSTPONED. CAROL BURNETT'S PREGNANT.

PREGNANT! HOW COULD SHE DO THAT TO ME?

SWEETHEART, DON'T TAKE IT PERSONALLY. *THESE THINGS HAPPEN!*

MARVIN, THE REASON I DIDN'T CALL YOU WAS LIZA AND I THOUGHT I SHOULD WAIT UNTIL I COULD LINE UP SOMETHING ELSE FOR US. LISTEN, I HAVE FABULOUS NEWS. THERE'S ANOTHER JULE STYNE SHOW. THERE'S A GIRL IN IT THAT IS SENSATIONAL. WE'LL BE STARTING IN THREE WEEKS. I NEED YOU TO BE MY ASSISTANT.

I WAS DAZED. I WAS TREMBLING.

I GOT A JOB ON A BROADWAY SHOW!

MARVIN, CUTIE, DID YOU HEAR ME? ARE YOU STILL THERE?

MARVIN, SWEETIE, ARE YOU *SURE* YOU'RE ALL RIGHT?

ASK HIM... WHAT'S THE NAME OF THE SHOW?

WHAT'S THE NAME OF THE SHOW, BUSTER?

IT'S CALLED... FUNNY GIRL!

SEPTEMBER ARRIVED AND REHEARSALS BEGAN. AND THANKS TO BUSTER, I STARTED TO LEARN THE WAY THE BROADWAY WORLD WORKS. THIS WAS THE REAL THING. WORKING BACKSTAGE. CRUMMY REHEARSAL HALLS, UP A FLIGHT OF STAIRS TO A BARREN ROOM WHERE THE RADIATOR IS THE COLDEST THING IN THE PLACE. THIS WAS "MARVIN, GET ME A CUPPA COFFEE." THIS WAS AN EDUCATION IN HARMONY, DIALOGUE, AND PRUNE DANISH. IF I THOUGHT I KNEW WHAT SHOW BUSINESS WAS ALL ABOUT BEFORE, I NOW KNEW I HAD A LOT TO LEARN.

I SAT ON THE PIANO BENCH NEXT TO BUSTER AS HE PLAYED FOR REHEARSALS AND TAUGHT THE CHORUS THE VOCAL ARRANGEMENTS AS THE SCORE CAME TO LIFE. HE WAS A DAMNED GOOD TEACHER.

FUNNY GIRL WAS A MUSICAL ABOUT FANNY BRICE, THE CLASSIC CLOWN OF THE ZIEGFELD FOLLIES. THE STAR OF OUR SHOW WAS A NEWCOMER NAMED *BARBRA STREISAND.*

I KNEW THAT BARBRA WOULD BE THE SUPERSTAR SHE HAS SINCE BECOME.

IT DIDN'T TAKE A JUILLIARD-TRAINED MUSICIAN TO KNOW THAT THIS WAS THE BEST VOICE ANYONE HAD HEARD IN *DECADES.*

GOOSE BUMPS SPRANG UP WHEN I ACCOMPANIED HER ON "PEOPLE".

FUNNY GIRL. IT HAD SO MUCH GOING FOR IT. FOR ONE THING, IT HAD THE STORY OF FANNY BRICE; FOR ANOTHER, IT HAD BARBRA STREISAND, THE TALENTED CLOWN WHO BECOMES A GLAMOROUS BROADWAY STAR. THE CINDERELLA STORY HAS ALWAYS HAD A SPECIAL APPEAL IN THE THEATER.

OF COURSE, I FELT AS IF I WERE LIVING THE CINDERELLA STORY MYSELF. *FUNNY GIRL* WAS A BLESSING, AND BUSTER DAVIS WAS NOTHING LESS THAN A *SAINT.*

IT IS ONE THING TO LEARN SOMETHING IN A CLASSROOM; IT'S ANOTHER TO EXPERIENCE IT LIVE.

MY ABILITY TO PLAY A SONG IN ANY KEY ON DEMAND WAS PROVING INVALUABLE. JULE STYNE WOULD SIT AT THE PIANO AND RUN THROUGH SOME CHANGES HE WANTED TO MAKE. I COULD INSTANTLY PLAY BACK WHAT I HEARD.

WHEN I WAS NOT POUNDING THE PIANO, I WAS A JUNIOR UNDERLING, A GOFER, AND MAN OF ALL WORK. FOR EXAMPLE, BARBRA STREISAND LOVED A KIND OF CHOCOLATE-COVERED DOUGHNUT, SO...

YET DESPITE OUR OPTIMISM, THE SHOW THAT HAD LOOKED SO PROMISING IN REHEARSAL RAN INTO PROBLEMS. SCENES FELT LONGISH. THE SCRIPT LACKED IMMEDIACY, AND THE WHISPERS STARTED: "WE NEED MORE BARBRA." IT WAS LIKE SAYING: "JUST GIVE THE BALL TO MICHAEL JORDAN." SOME OF THE SONGS DIDN'T WORK. WE WERE SO MESMERIZED BY BARBRA'S VOICE THAT WE HARDLY NOTICED THAT SOME OF THEM WEREN'T SERVING THE STORY. JULE STYNE AND BOB MERRILL STRUGGLED TO REWRITE THE SCORE.

MARVIN, LET'S TRY THIS ONE!

MARVIN, WE'VE GOT ANOTHER ONE.

MARVIN

MARVIN!

MARVIN!

MARVIN!

I MUST HAVE BEEN FED BRAND-NEW SONGS EVERY WEEK. IT WAS EXHAUSTING, BUT IT WAS THE BEST LEARNING EXPERIENCE I COULD HAVE ASKED FOR.

SCRIBBLE!

SCRIBBLE!

THE AUDIENCE AT THE OPENING IN BOSTON AT THE SHUBERT THEATER WENT WILD FOR STREISAND, BUT THEN ONE OF THE STRANGEST THINGS HAPPENED DURING THE SECOND ACT. PEOPLE STARTED LEAVING IN DROVES. NOT JUST A FEW PEOPLE. AN ENTIRE AUDIENCE. IT WAS AS IF WORD WERE SPREADING OF A BOMB THREAT. WERE WE SITTING ON A DISASTER? WHY WERE THEY LEAVING? WHAT HAD WE DONE TO LOSE AN ENTIRE AUDIENCE? THE CLEANING LADY FINALLY POINTED OUT THAT WE HAD BROKEN THE GOLDEN RULE OF BOSTON THEATER. WE HAD TO GET THE CURTAIN DOWN, BEFORE THEY SHUT DOWN THE TRANSIT SYSTEM! *FUNNY GIRL* WAS STRETCHING TO ALMOST FOUR HOURS, AND THE *LAST TRAIN WAS AT 11:45.*

A FULL TWENTY MINUTES WERE LOPPED OFF THE SHOW. I LEARNED A VERY IMPORTANT LESSON: *NEVER* TAKE AN AUDIENCE *FOR GRANTED.*

WHILE THE CAST REHEARSED DURING THE MORNING AND AFTERNOON, JULE, BOB, AND ISOBEL REWROTE AND REWROTE. THESE SESSIONS WENT ON INTO THE NIGHT.

I WAS POISED AT THE TELEPHONE IN MY HOTEL ROOM. ONCE JULE GAVE ME THE WORD, I WOULD COLLECT THE FRUITS OF HIS NIGHT'S LABOR.

HE ASKED ME TO TRANSCRIBE THE TAPE OF THE NEW MATERIAL AND REHEARSE WITH THE CAST.

ALTHOUGH THE SCRIPT WAS GETTING BETTER, THE ONE THING THAT NEVER CHANGED WAS THE RAVES FOR *BARBRA STREISAND.*

BARBRA WAS GIVEN TO CHANGING THE MELODY HERE OR THERE.

ONE EVENING AFTER THE SHOW, I GOT UP MY COURAGE AND WENT TO SEE BARBRA IN HER DRESSING ROOM. I TOLD HER THAT BY ALTERING A SONG, SHE WAS THROWING OFF THE MUSIC OF THE CHORUS.

MARVIN, WHAT ARE THESE PEOPLE PAYING MONEY TO HEAR— YOUR VOCAL ARRANGEMENTS?

THE NEXT NIGHT, I CHANGED THE BACKGROUND MUSIC.

ANOTHER RULE I LEARNED... WHEN IN TROUBLE, IF YOU CAN, GET YOURSELF JEROME ROBBINS, THE GREAT DIRECTOR AND CHOREOGRAPHER.

IN A FEW SHORT WEEKS, HE HAD PULLED THE WHOLE SHOW TOGETHER. IT WAS FINALLY "FROZEN" AND WOULD STAY THAT WAY.

MY WORK WAS COMPLETED. WHAT I DIDN'T REALIZE AT THE TIME WAS THAT ONCE A SHOW IS FROZEN, PEOPLE WHO ARE NOT ESSENTIAL TO THE PRODUCTION ARE LET GO.

COMPANY MANAGER

YOUR SERVICES ARE NO LONGER REQUIRED. YOU CAN GO HOME.

I TELEPHONED BUSTER AND TOLD HIM THE NEWS. I WAS HYSTERICAL.

SWEETHEART, I KNOW, I KNOW...

MARVIN. STAY THERE. I'LL CALL YOU RIGHT BACK.

TEN MINUTES LATER, JULE STYNE PHONED MY HOTEL ROOM.

I HAD BEEN REHIRED.

FUNNY GIRL OPENED AT THE WINTER GARDEN ON MARCH 26, 1964. THE MOMENT THE CURTAIN CAME DOWN, I RAN BACKSTAGE INTO THE MIDDLE OF THAT SPECIAL ELATION AND EUPHORIA THAT REIGN WHEN THERE'S NO DOUBT IN ANYONE'S MIND THAT YOU HAVE A *HIT*. I HAD TAKEN MY MOTHER WITH ME AND I BROUGHT HER BACKSTAGE. WHEN WE WALKED OUT THE STAGE DOOR...

...THERE WERE HUNDREDS OF PEOPLE WAITING FOR BARBRA TO APPEAR.

YOU SEE, MOM? YOU SEE WHAT THEY THINK OF THE *REHEARSAL PIANIST?*

BUSTER DAVIS COULDN'T HAVE BEEN KINDER OR A MORE TALENTED MENTOR. HE HAD STARTED IT ALL.

TO THIS DAY, I CAN STILL SAY THAT BUSTER WAS THE BEST ACCOMPANIST I HAD EVER SEEN.

BUSTER TOLD ME HE WAS ABOUT TO REPLACE HIS ASSISTANT ON THE *BELL TELEPHONE HOUR*, THE TV SHOW FOR WHICH HE WAS THE VOCAL ARRANGER. HE OFFERED ME THAT PRIZED POSITION.

JUGGLING SCHOOL, JUILLIARD, AND THIS DEMANDING JOB SEEMED IMPOSSIBLE. OF COURSE I ACCEPTED IMMEDIATELY.

THE BELL TELEPHONE HOUR WAS A MUSICAL JEWEL, WITH FOUR OR FIVE GUESTS ON EACH SHOW— EVERYONE FROM BROADWAY STARS TO OPERA DIVAS. IT GAVE ME THE CHANCE TO WORK WITH SOME OF THE *GREATEST*...

WHEN THE *BELL TELEPHONE HOUR* WENT OFF THE AIR A LITTLE BREATHING SPACE OPENED IN MY LIFE.

IT FELT STRANGE GOING TO COLLEGE WITHOUT DASHING BACK TO REHEARSALS.

HMM, SO THIS IS THE WAY *MOST KIDS* GO TO SCHOOL? INTERESTING!!

ANOTHER NICE THING ABOUT THIS QUIESCENT PERIOD WAS THAT MY STOMACHACHES HAD DISAPPEARED.

OUT OF THE BLUE, I GOT A CALL FROM A STRANGE LADY. SHE HAD GOTTEN MY NUMBER FROM ONE OF THE MUSICIANS IN *FUNNY GIRL*. THEY NEEDED A PIANO PLAYER FOR A PARTY THAT NIGHT. I REPLIED: "I'M A JUILLIARD MAN. I WAS THE REHEARSAL PIANIST FOR BARBRA STREISAND. I'VE WORKED ON THE BELL TELEPHONE HOUR. I'M A COMPOSER. I DO NOT PLAY PARTIES. REPEAT: *I DO NOT PLAY PARTIES!*

THAT'S TOO BAD, IT'S FOR *SAM SPIEGEL!*

I'LL BE THERE IN TWENTY MINUTES!

SAM SPIEGEL WAS THE PRODUCER OF *LAWRENCE OF ARABIA*, *ON THE WATERFRONT*, AND OTHER BLOCKBUSTERS.

I RACED FROM THE HOUSE TO SAM SPIEGEL'S SUITE AT THE ST. MORITZ HOTEL.

AS I BEGAN MY FOUR HOURS AT THE KEYBOARD, I WATCHED THE PLACE FILL UP WITH *SHOW-BUSINESS NOTABLES*.

HAROLD ROME ARRIVED, AND I QUICKLY PLAYED A MEDLEY OF HIS SONGS FROM *WISH YOU WERE HERE*; BETTY COMDEN AND ADOLPH GREEN APPEARED, AND I WENT INTO A MEDLEY OF THEIR SONGS FROM *ON THE TOWN* AND *BELLS ARE RINGING*. FAYE DUNAWAY ARRIVED AMID A GROUP OF *HOLLYWOOD 'A' LISTERS*.

EVEN *BOBBY KENNEDY*, WHO WAS RUNNING FOR A SEAT IN THE U.S. SENATE FROM NEW YORK, MADE AN APPEARANCE.

I SENSED THAT SAM SPIEGEL WAS VERY HAPPY THAT NIGHT. HE WAS USING A LIVE PIANO PLAYER FOR THE FIRST TIME.

THAT WAS GREAT! WHAT DO YOU DO BESIDES PLAY FOR PARTIES?

WELL, MR. SPIEGEL, IF THIS HADN'T BEEN YOUR PARTY, I WOULD NOT HAVE TAKEN THE JOB. I AM A... A *COMPOSER!*

SPIEGEL PROUDLY TOLD ME THAT HE HAD GIVEN *LEONARD BERNSTEIN* HIS BIG BREAK WHEN HE HIRED HIM TO WRITE THE SCORE FOR *ON THE WATERFRONT.*

I'VE GOT A NEW PICTURE, MARVIN, AND I'M LOOKING FOR SOMEBODY TO DO THE MUSIC. WHY DON'T YOU COME OVER AND PLAY FOR ME!

Burt Lancaster THE SWIMMER

SPIEGEL STUCK A COPY OF THE JOHN CHEEVER SHORT STORY IN MY COAT POCKET.

I DECIDED THAT BEFORE I MET WITH SPIEGEL, I WOULD HAVE THE MAIN THEME FOR THE SCORE FOR *THE SWIMMER* READY TO GO.

A FEW DAYS LATER, SPIEGEL CALLED. I APPEARED AT HIS HOTEL AND ANNOUNCED GRANDLY THAT I WAS NOT GOING TO PLAY ANY OF MY OLD SONGS FOR HIM.

WHAT DO YOU MEAN?

MR. SPIEGEL, I'M HERE TO PLAY YOU THE THEME FROM *THE SWIMMER!*

WHEN I FINISHED...

PLAY IT AGAIN, KID.

WHEN I FINISHED PLAYING IT A SECOND TIME, SPIEGEL GRABBED THE PHONE AND BEGAN CALLING A SUCCESSION OF PEOPLE. HE LOVED IT.

YOU'VE GOT TO HEAR THIS!

OVER THE NEXT FEW HOURS I MUST HAVE PLAYED IT AT LEAST FIFTEEN TIMES. WHEN THE LAST LISTENER HAD COME AND GONE, SPIEGEL CONFRONTED ME.

"OKAY, THAT'S IT. I WANT YOU TO DO THE MOVIE."

THEN SPIEGEL FROWNED.

"BUT CAN YOU DO A PICTURE? DO YOU KNOW WHAT IT TAKES TO SCORE A MOVIE?"

I LOOKED HIM STRAIGHT IN THE EYE...

SURE I DO!!

THE TRUTH WAS THAT I DIDN'T KNOW THE FIRST THING ABOUT THE MOVIE BUSINESS. I KNEW NOTHING ABOUT 35-MM FILM OR CLICK TRACKS.

...OR ALL THE THOUSAND AND ONE THINGS YOU HAVE TO KNOW TO WRITE MUSIC FOR A FEATURE FILM.

IF THIS WERE A MOVIE, THE SCENE WOULD FADE OUT ON THE GRUFF PRODUCER EMBRACING THE NEOPHYTE COMPOSER AS THE MUSIC SWELLED AND THE END CREDITS ROLLED.

SAM SPIEGEL HAD A REPUTATION OF BEING TIGHT WITH A BUCK.

HE OFFERED ME **$ 2,500.**

I KNEW THAT COMPOSERS WERE GETTING ANYWHERE FROM $ 25,000 TO $ 70,000 FOR MOVIE SCORES.

$ 2,500 WAS DEFINITELY ON THE LOW SIDE.

DON'T GET ME WRONG. I KNEW OPPORTUNITY WAS KNOCKING. STILL, IT SEEMED UNFAIR TO WRITE SIXTY MINUTES OF MUSIC FOR EIGHTY-FIVE MUSICIANS FOR A MULTI-MILLION-DOLLAR MOVIE FOR $ 2,500. YOU'D PAY THAT FOR A REFRIGERATOR WITH AN ICE MAKER. ON THE OTHER SIDE I HAD READ HORROR STORIES ABOUT ARTISTS WHO FOULED UP THEIR CAREERS FOR YEARS BY ASKING FOR A FEW DOLLARS MORE.

I DECIDED TO ASK QUINCY JONES.

IT SEEMS LIKE A LOT OF WORK FOR THAT AMOUNT OF MONEY. I MADE FIFTEEN HUNDRED A WEEK AS A REHEARSAL PIANIST FOR THE TELEPHONE HOUR.

YOU'RE RIGHT, MARVIN. YOU CAN'T ACCEPT THAT, TELL SPIEGEL TO FORGET IT. **WALK.** IT'S SLAVE LABOR!

I DECIDED TO HAVE MY LAWYER SAY I WANTED MORE MONEY. FINALLY, I WAS OFFERED, AND ACCEPTED **$ 7,500.**

A FEW DAYS LATER, TWENTY REELS OF FILM AND SOUND TRACK WERE DELIVERED.

I HAD TO RENT A MOVIOLA, THAT LETS YOU VIEW A REEL OF 35-MM FILM ON A TINY SCREEN. TWO HUGE MEN WRESTLED THIS GIANT MACHINE UP THE STAIRS TO OUR APARTMENT.

DRRRRRR!

I PUT THE MOVIOLA AT A RIGHT ANGLE TO MY PIANO KEYBOARD. I HAD TO TIME EACH SEGMENT WITH A STOPWATCH. THAT WAS EASY, THANKS TO MY SESSIONS WITH DR. STOPWATCH.

CUCK!

WHEN YOU'RE WRITING THE MUSIC FOR A MOVIE, 50 TO 55 PERCENT IS IN THE QUALITY OF THE MUSIC YOU CREATE, YOUR INSPIRATION AND TALENT. BUT THERE'S A TREMENDOUS AMOUNT OF WORK THAT IS PURELY CALCULATING **MINUTES** AND **SECONDS**.

RRRRR

CUCK!

YOU CAN WRITE THE GREATEST MINUTE AND THIRTY SECONDS, BUT IF THEY ONLY NEED A MINUTE TWENTY-EIGHT, YOU HAVEN'T DONE THE JOB. I COULDN'T HELP BUT THINK THAT IF FRÉDÉRIC CHOPIN HAD WRITTEN THE "MINUTE WALTZ" AND BROUGHT IT TO SAM SPIEGEL, HE MIGHT HEAR SAM SAY: "FREDDY, I LOVE IT, IT'S CATCHY. BUT WE ONLY NEED FIFTY-EIGHT SECONDS. GO HOME AND TRY AGAIN." THAT'S THE MECHANICAL PART OF MOTION-PICTURE SCORING. THE OTHER IS MORE IMPORTANT: THE CREATIVE DECISIONS ON WHAT KIND OF MUSIC AND WHERE IT WILL GO.

HE ONLY NEEDS FIFTY-EIGHT SECONDS??

IN JOHN WILLIAMS'S SCORE FOR JAWS— WITH ALL THOSE LOW BASSES— I STILL DON'T FEEL IT'S SAFE TO GO BACK INTO THE WATER.

THERE ARE ALTERNATIVES AS TO WHAT TO HIGHLIGHT IN ANY GIVEN SCENE. FOR EXAMPLE, IN A CHASE SCENE THE COMPOSER CAN SIMPLY ACCENTUATE THE CHASE AND PROVIDE ACCELERATED MUSIC.

OR HE CAN MIRROR THE FEAR OF THE CHARACTERS WHO ARE ON THE RUN WITH "FEAR MUSIC."

I CONTINUED ON THE SCORE FOR WEEKS, WORKING NIGHT AND DAY. MY MOTHER LOVED IT, BUT SHE TENDED TO LOVE EVERYTHING I WROTE. MY FATHER LIKED IT, TOO. HE SAW IN THE SERIOUS, SYMPHONIC SOUND OF MY SCORE THAT MAYBE MY JUILLIARD YEARS WERE PAYING OFF.

IT IS USUAL FOR A *WISE* COMPOSER TO PHONE HIS PRODUCER FROM TIME TO TIME AND PLAY A FEW FRESHLY MINTED PIECES OF MUSIC FOR HIM. JUST TO KEEP IN TOUCH. TO LET HIM KNOW HE IS GETTING HIS *MONEY'S WORTH.*

A FEW WEEKS INTO MY WORK, SAM SPIEGEL PHONES ME. HE IS RAGING MAD. NOT JUST A LITTLE PERTURBED; I'M TALKING *VOLCANIC ANGRY.*

WHY HAVEN'T I HEARD ANYTHING YET? WHAT THE HELL'S GOING ON?

HE DIDN'T REALIZE THAT I ALREADY HAD ALMOST HALF THE PICTURE DONE. I PROMISED TO RUSH RIGHT OVER TO HIS APARTMENT AND PLAY WHAT I'D WRITTEN.

I GOT TO HIS SUITE AND PLAYED THE MUSIC FOR THE FIRST FOUR REELS. SPIEGEL CALMED DOWN AND TURNED INTO THE CHARMING MAN I KNEW. HE LOVED THE MUSIC.

AND SO THE CRISIS PASSED. OR SO I THOUGHT. A FEW DAYS LATER, MY PHYSICAL SYSTEM JUST ABOUT BROKE DOWN, AND MY DOCTOR ORDERED A BATTERY OF TESTS ON MY STOMACH. I WAS GIVEN AN UPPER GI SERIES, WHICH PROVED NEGATIVE. BUT THE TERRIBLE STOMACH PAINS CONTINUED INTERMITTENTLY, AND SOME OF THEM HAD ME DOUBLING OVER. I WAS TOLD TO TAKE MORE LIQUID MAALOX AND TRY TO GET MORE REST. WELL, I DIDN'T KNOW THE MEANING OF THE WORD *REST.* PANIC, YES; REST, NO. IT JUST WASN'T MY STYLE.

I FINISHED THE SCORE, AND LUCKILY THE PAINS SUBSIDED...

IT WAS TIME TO FLY TO...

HOLLYWOOD

I HAD HIRED TWO OF HOLLYWOOD'S BEST ORCHESTRATORS TO DO THE FILM. THEY WERE JACK HAYES AND LEO SHUKEN. I HAD ORIGINALLY PLANNED TO CONDUCT THE SCORE MYSELF, THOUGH I HAD NEVER DONE IT BEFORE. A WORD OF ADVICE TO ARTISTS IN TRAINING: LEARN ALL YOU CAN TO PREPARE YOURSELF FOR THE CHALLENGES OF LIFE. BUT WHEN YOU FIND YOURSELF FACING THE *UNKNOWN*, DON'T BE AFRAID TO ASK FOR HELP.

THE SWIMMER

THE SWIMMER FINALLY OPENED IN THE SUMMER OF 1968.

THOUGH THE FILM ITSELF DID NOT DO TOO WELL, MY SCORE GOT SOME MARVELOUS REVIEWS, PARTICULARLY IN THE *HOLLYWOOD REPORTER* AND *VARIETY*.

THE SWIMMER BROUGHT ME ANOTHER JOB ALMOST AT ONCE. I WAS ABOUT TO TAKE IT WHEN I WAS FELLED BY ANOTHER ONE OF MY TERRIFIC STOMACHACHES. I WAS DIAGNOSED WITH A BLEEDING ULCER.

I WAS SURE THE ENTIRE MUSICAL COMMUNITY THOUGHT OF ME AS A "SICKIE."

BUT THE TELEPHONE RANG. THIS TIME IT WAS AN OFFER TO SCORE A FILM FOR *WOODY ALLEN*. A WOODY ALLEN FILM? ME, MARVIN HAMLISCH? OF COURSE I SAID YES.

I HAD BEEN ASKED TO WRITE THE SCORE FOR THE FIRST FILM THAT HE BOTH WROTE AND DIRECTED: *TAKE THE MONEY AND RUN*.

BEFORE I MET WOODY, I THOUGHT: I'LL BE ROLLING ON THE FLOOR, LAUGHING ALL THE TIME. WELL, NOT QUITE. WOODY WAS VERY QUIET WHEN I MET HIM. HE WAS QUIET WHEN I WORKED FOR HIM. HE WAS QUIET WHEN I RECORDED THE MUSIC FOR *TAKE THE MONEY AND RUN* AND THEN FOR *BANANAS*. LATER HE HARDLY EVER USED A COMPOSER FOR HIS FILMS AGAIN. I SOMETIMES WONDER IF WORKING WITH *ME* PUT THAT IDEA INTO HIS HEAD.

THE NEXT MOVIE I WAS OFFERED WAS *KOTCH*, A SORT OF GERIATRIC COMEDY STARRING WALTER MATTHAU AND DIRECTED BY HIS FRIEND JACK LEMMON.

JACK WANTED A TITLE SONG— FINALLY, MY CHANCE FOR A HIT. WE MANAGED TO GET *JOHNNY MERCER* TO WRITE THE LYRICS.

HE DID WHAT NO OTHER LYRICIST I EVER WORKED WITH HAD EVER DONE-- COME UP WITH FIVE DIFFERENT SETS OF LYRICS; FIVE COMPLETE VERSIONS OF THE SONG, EACH PERFECTLY MARRIED TO THE MELODY.

KOTCH CAME OUT, AND IT WASN'T A HUGE SUCCESS AT THE BOX OFFICE, THOUGH IT DID RESPECTABLE BUSINESS. I HAD HALF-FORGOTTEN ABOUT IT. THEN, ON A FEBRUARY MORNING IN 1972, I RECEIVED A LETTER. I WAS ASTONISHED. I WAS SHOCKED. I WAS NOMINATED FOR A *GOLDEN GLOBE* AWARD FOR *KOTCH*!

THE EVENING ARRIVED FOR THE GOLDEN GLOBES. OUR MOVIE HAD RECEIVED QUITE A FEW NOMINATIONS. BUT TO EVERYONE'S DISMAY, WE WERE LOSING IN ONE CATEGORY AFTER ANOTHER...

MARVIN, IF YOU DON'T WIN, I'M GOING TO KILL YOU!

BECAUSE WE'VE GOT TO HAVE A PARTY, AND IN ORDER TO HAVE A PARTY, YOU'VE GOT TO ACTUALLY **WIN** SOMETHING!

WHY??

AND THEN I HEAR A VOICE IN MY RIGHT EAR:

"THE WINNER IS 'LIFE IS WHAT YOU MAKE IT' BY JOHNNY MERCER AND **MARVIN HAMLISCH.**"

I WAS BEING SMOTHERED BY JACK'S KISSES, AND I STUMBLED TOWARD THE STAGE.

I HAD NO SPEECH PREPARED. I WAS SO STUNNED I DOUBTED I COULD TALK, ANYWAY. NEVERTHELESS THEY TELL ME IT WAS PROBABLY THE LONGEST SPEECH IN THE HISTORY OF THE GOLDEN GLOBES.

CAN LIGHTNING STRIKE TWICE? I COULDN'T BELIEVE IT, BUT A COUPLE OF WEEKS LATER WE WE WERE NOMINATED FOR AN *ACADEMY AWARD*. I WAS ON THE EDGE OF MY CHAIR, AS I HEARD THE WORDS: "AND THE WINNER IS '*SHAFT*.'"

THE ONLY THING I COULD THINK ABOUT WAS THAT I WAS A LOSER. IT HAS TAKEN ME A LIFETIME TO REALIZE THAT IT'S IN THE *DOING* THAT WE RECEIVE THE SATIS-FACTION OF KNOWING WE'VE DONE OUR BEST, NOT IN THE ADULATION. WASN'T THIS REALLY WHAT MY FATHER HAD WANTED ME TO LEARN— THAT MY MUSIC DID NOT NEED TO WIN AN AWARD, BUT RATHER, TO BE TRUE TO ITSELF AND WORTHY? THAT WAS THE GOAL TO STRIVE FOR. I CAN STILL HONESTLY SAY THAT I *NEVER COMPROMISED*.

I THINK I OWE THAT KIND OF MUSICAL INTEGRITY TO THOSE *FIFTY MINUTES ON THE ROOF* AND MY *TEACHERS AT JUILLIARD*.

EPILOGUE

HER NAME WAS FRANCES S. GOLDSTEIN. SHE WAS AN IRASCIBLE OLD WOMAN WHO ALWAYS HAD A CIGARETTE IN HER MOUTH.

SHE WAS TOUGH, BUT SHE TAUGHT ME MORE ABOUT MUSIC THEORY THAN ANYONE BEFORE OR SINCE.

IF MISS GOLDSTEIN SAID YOU HAD DONE WELL, IT WASN'T SAID LIGHTLY TO REASSURE YOU. YOU *HAD* DONE WELL.

I DEARLY WANTED HER APPROVAL NOW. WITH ALL THAT WAS HAPPENING TO ME, I NEEDED HER TO REASSURE ME I WAS ON THE RIGHT TRACK. AND WANTED HER TO SEE THAT I WAS CAPABLE OF DOING SERIOUS WORK.

MISS GOLDSTEIN, I'D LOVE TO HAVE YOU LISTEN TO THE MUSIC I WROTE. I REALLY THINK IT'S *GOOD*.

MARVIN, I DON'T HAVE TIME TO LISTEN TO THIS MUSIC OF YOURS. I'M VERY, *VERY* BUSY.

YEARS LATER, I VISITED MISS GOLDSTEIN IN THE HOSPITAL. SHE HAD CANCER AND WAS NOT EXPECTED TO LIVE. AS I LOOKED DOWN AT HER FRAIL BODY IN THE HOSPITAL BED, IT WAS HARD TO RECALL THE TEACHER WHO SEEMED SO TOUGH AND FORMIDABLE AT JUILLIARD. SHE TOLD ME THAT HER STUDENTS DIDN'T VISIT HER, AND THIS DID NOT SURPRISE ME. SHE WAS A KILLER IN THE CLASSROOM AND NOT IMMENSELY LIKABLE. NOW SHE COULD BARELY SPEAK. THOSE EVER-PRESENT CIGARETTES HAD RAVAGED HER THROAT. WE TALKED OF THE OLD DAYS AT JUILLIARD AND OF MY NEW CAREER. FINALLY, IT WAS *TIME TO GO*.

MARVIN...

YES, MISS GOLDSTEIN?

I REALLY SHOULD HAVE *TAKEN TIME* TO LISTEN TO YOUR MUSIC...

!

THE END.